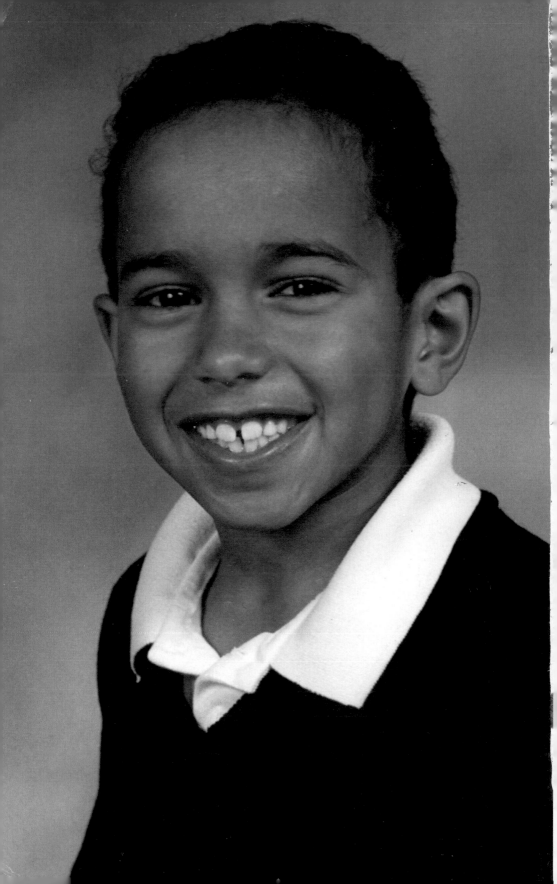

LEWIS HAMILTON

LEWIS HAMILTON

MY STORY

HarperSport
An Imprint of HarperCollinsPublishers

First published in 2007 by
HarperSport
an imprint of HarperCollins
London

© Lewis Hamilton 2007

1

A CIP catalogue record for this book is
available from the British Library

HB ISBN 13 978-0-00-727005-7
HB ISBN 10 0-00-727005-4
PB ISBN 13 978-0-00-727093-4
PB ISBN 10 0-00-727093-3

Printed and bound in Great Britain by
Clays Ltd, St Ives plc

The HarperCollins website address is:
www.harpercollins.co.uk

To the people who made this all possible
To my family, to McLaren and to Mercedes-Benz

CONTENTS

ACKNOWLEDGEMENTS

MY STORY IS, I HOPE, AN INSPIRATIONAL BOOK for those who want to know more about me and how I made it to Formula One. It is the story of my first year in Grand Prix racing and aspects of my life from the very beginning, from karting aged eight through winning in GP2 aged 21 to my incredible jump to a Vodafone McLaren Mercedes Formula One race seat aged 22.

Although I can remember everyone who has helped me in my career so far, it would be impossible to name them all in this book as it is an account of my career to date rather than an autobiography of my life – I'm too young for that!

For now, I would like to say a huge thank you to you all.

A special thank you also to my family and friends, to McLaren and Mercedes-Benz and to publishers HarperCollins for their help and support in putting this book together.

Finally, I am grateful to Timothy Collings and his team for assisting me with the writing of *My Story*.

Lewis Hamilton, *October 2007*

CHAPTER

RESOLVE

'That I led the championship from the third race
of the season all the way to the last was an
amazing feat in itself, even if it meant the final
outcome was tinged with some
disappointment. I soon got over
that, though ...'

MY STORY IS NOT ABOUT LUCK OR A FAIRY TALE. It is about hard work, about my family's sacrifices and determination, my dad's huge support for me and many other people's belief and kindness. I found I had a talent and I have worked as hard as possible to develop it so that I can be successful and in the process inspire others, if I can, to achieve a dream.

It has been an unbelievable year, easily the most exciting and challenging of my life. From the start in Melbourne, which seems so long ago now, to the finish in São Paulo, I travelled through a phenomenal Formula One year, winning four races, finishing as runner-up in five, and battling for podium finishes in a few others, in my rookie season with the Vodafone McLaren Mercedes team.

That I led the championship from the third race of the season all the way to the last was an amazing feat in itself, even if it meant the final outcome was tinged with some disappointment. I soon got over that, though – thanks to my dad's endless positive energy and example, and the McLaren team's great spirit, not to mention a memorable team party organized by Vodafone on the Sunday night after that final race at Interlagos. It summed up our unity at the end of a very trying season and I admit I enjoyed the opportunity to let my hair down a bit with my friends and team-mates. Shoot, it was worth it! I ended the season with good vibes. I felt proud of the team for the way they had worked through to the end of a really difficult, troubled year. The São Paulo party was good for us all. Ron Dennis made a speech and said some really good things and we had a great evening. It just rounded off the whole year and, when I was mentioned a couple of times, it made me feel proud to be part of that team.

So much happened to me in such a short a space of time that, when the season ended, I felt like I needed to stop, look back and take stock of what had happened. But in Formula One there is no time for that. The search for progress is relentless, the appetite for success, improvement and frontier-breaking unquenchable. Stand still for a moment and your rivals will pass you. *Whoooosh!* That is the competitive nature of the sport. It comes out in every aspect of all of the teams' activities. Nothing is left to chance, no stone left unturned, in pursuit of greater speed, efficiency and effectiveness in all areas of a racing team. And that restlessness reflects the way I have always felt about my life in racing. I always want to move on and on, to keep going forward to the next level and the next challenge. But I always want to succeed properly, fair and square, out on the track and not in any other way.

I had arrived in São Paulo leading the championship by four points, but I left in second place, just a single point behind the new champion Kimi Räikkönen. I may have been hit by mechanical problems, but I was beaten fair and square on the Interlagos track by Kimi and his Ferrari. It was no time for recriminations or complaints. I do not believe in doing that; I do not blame my team when things happen. We all win and lose together. Kimi drove superbly and won six races in all, including three out of the final four Grands Prix. He deserved his success. That is why I was quick to congratulate him at the end of the race in the *parc fermé*. I felt sore for myself, but I felt happy for Kimi – he is a cool guy and he has been a great competitor this year.

I had just finished my rookie year at the age of 22. I knew I had a future in Formula One and, with reasonable luck, plenty more opportunities to win the World Championship. I had no doubt about that. It had been a fantastic season and instead of feeling down, or in any kind of pain, I felt we had a lot to celebrate and enjoy. I felt proud of the way the team had come through a sometimes stormy, controversial year and I felt proud, too, of my family and all my friends and supporters who had helped me to get where I was, so close to the title in my first season. It was a day to be happy. In the end, the year was not decided by that one race in Brazil, but a whole championship season.

It was also one of the most exciting Formula One seasons ever, at least on the track. If somebody had told me a year ago that I would be fighting for the World Championship at the end of the 2007 season, I would have said they were dreaming. But that is what happened. In the end, I lost by just one point, but I proved I had the potential to be involved in more and more championship fights in the future. Nobody would have predicted that I would finish second in my first season, so there was no reason for anything but celebrations. I did my best, the team did their best and there was nothing any of us could do to change things. In all honesty, at the end, I just felt it had been a really intense, crazy year and, truly, I did not feel gutted by the outcome. It was cool. I believed and still believe in the team and the car, and I am looking ahead with real optimism.

Who would have thought I would be leading the World Championship going into the last race? Who could have imagined the crowds we had at Silverstone for the British Grand Prix? Who would have dreamt that I would go to North America and win back-to-back Grands Prix in Canada and the United States? Or win four races and start from pole position six times in 17 races?

I know it was all against me in the end, and that the final two races were bad results for me, but I plan to learn from that and to go into next year and try to improve all round. I am

going to come back fitter, more relaxed and more experienced
– and I will have a better car and I will push harder for the
championship. To think I came straight from GP2 to be ranked
number two in the world is a positive thing and I know we
will be strong next year. We will do a better job, for sure, the
team will keep pushing and I have got the experience now and
I will bank that. I cannot wait for the next race! Of course, I
felt emotional afterwards in Brazil, at least a little bit. I try not
to show emotions, but I cannot deny that I felt it a little when
the season ended.

When I think back, there are so many great memories: my
GP2 Championship, then the opportunity to test for the Vodafone McLaren Mercedes team and those early tests at Silverstone and at Jerez in September and October 2006. They were
just a year before the title-decider in Brazil. I remember that
first week of testing at Silverstone when I wore some other
dude's race suit to start with, and it smelt. When I got my own,
I thought it was so cool, I wanted to sleep in it! The whole
journey for me, from my earliest days as part of the McLaren
and Mercedes Benz family to Formula One, has been quite
emotional. And this last year has been a rollercoaster.

The test at Silverstone – only a year before I flew to Japan
and China for the two Grands Prix that lifted me within reach
of the title and then dashed my hopes – was the best week of
my life at the time. I enjoyed it so much. I felt the pressure,
because it was my first test, but it was so cool. I worked my
way through it. The thing that really struck me, after GP2, was

the downforce in the high-speed corners. I was like, 'Wow, this is Formula One! I want this!' And then I went to Jerez to test again, and gradually, after not such a fast start, I was into it and doing the laps. I just loved that testing and it went well and, looking back now, I have only good memories.

It seems so long ago. So, too, does the day I was confirmed as Fernando's team-mate, as a race driver in the team, and all the other testing. And the launch in Valencia on 15 January earlier in the year, when we did all the razzmatazz and had those huge crowds and did the 'doughnuts' in the streets . . . So much has happened since – and luckily for me, nearly all of it has been good. One of the few bad days came when I had a big accident testing the new MP4-22 at Valencia in January before the season. Fortunately for me I was unhurt, but the car was quite badly damaged and it set us back in our test programme. That accident was a shaker for me, a reminder of what these cars can do and it was a big part of my early learning experience with the team.

In fact I have learned something every day in this last year. I am so competitive that I always want to achieve more and more. It is a positive force for me. I want to win. You have to be realistic and remember this was my first season and that it was something special for me. I was bound to make some mistakes. I started out just hoping to learn a lot, to challenge Fernando and to prove I was worth my seat in the team. The level of expectation was a measure of how far I had gone in that space of time.

After Brazil, I was asked if there was anything different I would do for next season given my experiences this year. A lot of things, really. Now after one season in Formula One, I have the experience to know how to plan my year differently so I can be more structured and have more time for myself and for my family. Next year I will know the circuits, apart from the new ones – and they are street circuits so I love them anyway. It is not so much about doing things differently but doing them better. I want to be fitter, work harder and be a better driver all round. I know all of this is not something that can be achieved in one year, as it takes time to evolve – especially if you are striving to become the best in the world. My dream is still there and it is still in front of me. So in one way, maybe it is a good thing that I have not been crowned number one this year, because there is a long time to come in my life and I am sure I will have a lot more opportunities.

I find it easy to overcome disappointments and negativity. Life goes on and every new day is a new positive. Sometimes, you just have to say to yourself, 'Get on with it.' I am my own biggest critic and often want to say, 'Lewis, kick it!' I push myself. It is the same for us all in the team and we work for each other, helping one another as much as we can. A racing team is not just about the person who is driving the car. It is much, much bigger than that. I have been very lucky this year to have learned a lot from the Vodafone McLaren Mercedes team. I have gained so much from driving and handling the car, set-up, tyre selection, strategy and the whole range of factors that can make a driver successful.

I have also learned a lot about the politics of Formula One . . .

CHAPTER

INSPIRATIONS

'Dad is my biggest supporter, and a fantastic father, without whom I may not have even discovered I had any talent for racing.'

TO BE A FORMULA ONE RACING DRIVER you need to be extremely fit and prepared – both physically and mentally – for the whole challenge. It is far more exhausting than you can ever imagine if you have never raced in a car. And it is not easy. Sometimes, if you are not feeling right, if you do not have the right energy levels, it can be impossible. It is important to find your own way, then keep your mind clear and maintain the right level of motivation.

Just the ordinary things – like travelling all the time; packing bags, grabbing them and taking them with you; going to functions, meeting people; the crowds, the heavy schedule – all take their toll on your energy and strength after a while. So it is important to stay calm when you can and not to waste energy.

I have a special source of extra motivation. For me, even when I am feeling pretty stretched, rushing around in the middle of a Formula One weekend and surrounded by people who want a bit of my time – and with what feels like a thousand things to do – I only have to think of one person to keep me feeling motivated and to put a smile on my face: my brother Nicolas. I remember Linda, my step-mum, being pregnant with Nic. I remember him being born and that I would just go and sit next to him and watch him. I had prayed to have a brother and was so happy when he came into the world. It really meant a lot to me, in my childhood, to have a brother. And it still does.

Nic was born two months early and it was a long time after his birth – I think nearly eighteen months – before he was diagnosed with cerebral palsy. He was still the same Nic to us and we loved him whatever. Nic has trouble walking, and this affects his whole body to a point, but he never complains. He always has a smile on his face whatever the situation.

I remember when Nic was four he had to have an operation on his legs to extend the tendons so as to increase his mobility. The operation was a major one and very distressing. Nic had to have cuts in his groin, behind his knees, and in his ankles. He was in plaster for about eight weeks. I was only eleven and heavily into my karting by then, going to race tracks at weekends and having a great time. We always went to every race as a family – Linda, Nic, my dad and me. Nic was let out of hospital after about a week and they gave him this little wheelchair. As soon as he was released, Nic was back on the racing circuit with us, his legs stretched out straight in

front of him and plastered up to the groin. The whole operation period was a very traumatic time for us all, in particular
Nic, who, when the time came to take off his plaster casts,
thought the doctors were going to cut his legs off. I remember
he cried his eyes out but it wasn't long before that smile came
back to his face. That smile – it is infectious and inspirational.
It taught me a lot about life. Nic has always been my number
one fan and I am his.

I just hope that by writing about him, he doesn't get too
big-headed because, if he does, I will have to make sure he
soon forgets it! He is such a character, so grounded too, and he
is always cheerful and happy. He has big respect from me and
all who know him. Nic is seven years younger than me and
because of that, I sometimes feel like I have to teach him
things, like my dad did for me. But most of the time, I am
learning stuff from him.

Nic is now fifteen and, if anything, we are even closer. I
love spending time with him. We enjoy the same sort of
things, the same sort of music. As he gets older, it's good to be
able to talk about girls with him! It won't be long before we
can go partying together – and I am dying for the time when
he is old enough so we can go out to a club or just do our own
thing. That is going to be so cool.

It is rare for me during the season to get a decent period of
time at my parents' home to spend with Nic but we did have a
few this year. After the Turkish Grand Prix, for example, and
before I had to travel to Italy, I went home to my parents'

house in Hertfordshire. The weather was great, Nic was there and we had fun doing all kinds of things together.

We played golf one day, for example. Nic finds it extremely difficult to stand still and balance in one place; add to that the fact that he is also left-handed, which does not help his swing. Even though he shouldn't be able to, Nic still attempts to play football, basketball, almost everything. He just never gives up and always puts 100 per cent effort into trying something even if he knows it's too much for him. Nic gets out of life what he puts into life and that must give him a huge amount of satisfaction. I know that he cannot do things as well as me but he has a real good go at it and makes me work even harder to make sure I beat him. 'Never let him have it easy,' is what my dad always said, just so that he would try harder. I am lucky in that I am good at most sports, but for Nic it must be really difficult. Either way, he always puts a smile on my face – although occasionally he can be quite argumentative. He reminds me of myself!

I often try to imagine myself in Nic's position. I do not think I would be anywhere near as strong as him. There's just so much to admire in him. So, whatever I am doing, I say to myself, 'If you think it's hard to do this, then think again.' I think about Nic's strength of character and that gives me added strength. So Nic is my inspiration – and that helps me a lot. But, in fact, my whole family are very close. We do everything we can together, and we always have done, but as I grow older and become more independent each year, I know that is probably going to change a bit – but not all that much. We have an intense bond and are a strong family. It helps us remain as normal as possible, to stay focused on the right things and not be distracted by all the stuff going on around us. We are a team, my family. We always have been. I like to think of my parents' home as my power station, the place where I can go to seek support, rest and reassurance in the good things in life.

Thanks to my family, I know it is important not to lose perspective – though at times in the past year, that has not been easy. Formula One is such a demanding and fast-moving business that it is easy to lose your own sense of direction sometimes. It can be very, very tough so you have to concentrate fully on the job in hand, prepare well and stay as level-headed and consistent as you can. If you stick to your beliefs and your true values in life, I believe things work out right in the end.

My mum Carmen and dad Anthony divorced when I was about two and I lived with my mum until I was ten. After that I moved to live with my dad and step-mum Linda. My mum is a huge and important part of my life and has always been there in the background wishing me success from afar. My step-mum Linda has been amazing and I think she is the best step-mum in the world. I was very emotionally attached to my dad, and it was difficult only seeing him at the weekends. They were the greatest weekends – I would not have missed them for anything – but I remember when I was ten that I liked living with my mum because she was the 'easier' parent.

You know with parents when you have the easy one and the demanding one? Well, she was the easier one. I've been extremely lucky: both my mum and Linda are incredibly considerate, very caring and generous, and fun-loving.

A huge part of my personality – the emotional side, I would say – comes from both my mums. Even though my dad always told me, 'You have to be polite,' that was already in my nature. I would say my stronger, more competitive side comes from my dad. My selfishness, my focus, my determination, my ability to put things out of my mind, the way I say things and express myself, present myself well, and everything that gives people their perception of you – that all comes from, and has been driven by, my dad.

For example, my approach to things is: do not waver, do not give up. My dad reminds me of that nearly every single day and I am always aware of how much work we have put in to get where we are today – and how much more work he expects me to do in the future! He is as relentless in his own way as I am in mine and I am sure that is a part of our characters that has contributed to our achievements. We are both hard workers and we believe in the same things – honesty, loyalty and trust – and we both have a never-say-die attitude. Anyone who knows him will tell you that. He is my biggest supporter, and a fantastic father, without whom I may not have even discovered I had any talent for racing! And he is a big reason – really the absolute reason – that I have been able to develop myself as a racing driver, and, probably more importantly, as a human being.

I am very close to my roots – to my father's family in Grenada, West Indies, where my real home is, and to the Grenadian people. My granddad lives in Grenada and drives a private minibus. His passengers are predominantly school children but my granddad will give just about anyone a lift. He is supposed to charge per ride but he just loves his job so much that sometimes he allows some passengers to ride for free. All the kids love him and out of respect they call him 'Uncle Dave', although his real name is Davidson. Nearly everyone in Grenada knows Uncle Dave. Wherever he goes people always acknowledge him and call out 'Uncle Dave!' He is everyone's uncle! My dad bought my granddad a new 18-seater minibus about a year ago because the old one was over twenty-five years old and my dad feared for the safety of my granddad and the passengers. I think my granddad's friends couldn't believe it. Some people didn't want to ride in Uncle Dave's old minibus because it was too slow but now everyone wants to ride in his new one.

I feel close to all of that. I love Grenada; it is a beautiful country and a place where I have learned a lot. Living in multicultural Europe, it is easy to take things for granted, while in Grenada some people still live in buildings that resemble sheds. We visit Grenada every year, sometimes twice a year, and during our visits I get a real perspective on things, a better understanding of life altogether – and I realize how blessed I am. My family, my roots, and our values are primarily Grenadian although we are British, having been born in the UK. My granddad came to England in the 1950s and then returned to Grenada in the seventies following the death of my grandmother. My dad has always expressed a wish to return and I plan to do the same at some stage in my life but not now. To see the kids in Grenada with smiles on their faces – even if they've got very, very little in comparison with European kids – helps me to understand and manage my way in life. So my principles are always to listen to my dad, cherish my family, compete hard and never give up. Most of all, I try to keep a smile on my face.

Alongside the great experiences in my life I've also had some very bad, really challenging times – which you will read about later – but even those have made me stronger. And, with the help of my family, I've bounced back twice as strong as before. I think that is why I am probably such a strong character in racing. Every mistake and every good thing that has happened to me has counted. And there is not a day gone by that I wished I had done more of this or that. The way I see it, you have to rise above things and move on. You just cannot wait around. You have to do it yourself and just get on with it if you want things to happen.

That is why I feel like I have got such a responsibility to make people happy, make younger kids more determined or ambitious and all that sort of thing. For me that is a pleasure:

it is not just about the racing; it is all those other things that come into it that I really, really enjoy. I do occasionally pray – my granddad is very religious, he goes to church every day and he is always on my case, asking, 'Are you praying?' or telling me, 'Not to worry, Lewis, the Lord will provide, just ask for His help.' Every now and then I will say a prayer and show my appreciation. I try to make sure it is not only when I am in trouble and I need help; even when I have had a great day, I try to thank God for it.

That is why religion is not an issue for me – any more than race is an issue. I am Roman Catholic; I was baptized when I was two and for a lot of my life I always thought there was something there. Sometimes, if I was in trouble I would pray, but I was never hardcore into it – but then neither was the family, although we all believe. I have always felt very much that I have been gifted and very much blessed – I have a great family, a talent which many people don't either get to discover or experience, and I really do feel like there is a higher power and that He has given me something. Whether it is to send a message out, or to use, or just to have fun, I do not know. I think everyone has got talent and gifts, but not everyone discovers them, and people can occasionally be misled. I am fortunate that I have not been. I feel everyone is put here for a purpose and all the individuals that do discover things in their life are able to make a change and make a difference.

Some people think race, or skin colour, is an issue; some think religion is. Putting it simply, I do not like to see anyone treated badly. I do not like people who do not behave well, who are not polite or who do not show respect when they should. I guess it comes from my own younger days when I had to do things and I didn't find it easy. I had a bad time at school because there were some bullies around who were probably jealous of me going karting at weekends; either that or they just didn't like me. I tried to deal with that by defending myself, so I learned karate. That is my way of sorting out my problems. I try not to get entangled, I prefer to rise above them, but sometimes you need to be able to stand your ground, don't you? I believe in doing things right and doing them properly.

I had a lot of other experiences when I was young, some good, some bad, but from each of them I learned something. In 1997, when I was thirteen, I went to my first Grand Prix at Spa-Francorchamps in Belgium. My dad and I were having a great day as guests of McLaren Mercedes. I remember walking around with my dad and we saw Eddie Irvine and decided to go and ask him for his autograph. I stood there in admiration of him, waiting for him to sign my book, but he looked at me and just walked on. It may well have been that Eddie was incredibly busy and did not have the time to be distracted or that he was just having a bad day. There are numerous reasons why this episode could have happened. At my age at that time, however, I didn't think of any of that but know what it's like now. I have never forgotten how that made me feel.

Someone else showed me how different it can be. That was David Coulthard. I also met him at Spa. I was standing at the front of the McLaren garage when David came in and walked straight past me and my dad. I called out, 'Alright, David?' and he turned round and, two seconds later, he said, 'Alright, Lewis?' He knew me . . . what a feeling that was! He had come to see me karting and he remembered me. I really appreciated it. So, always, I have huge respect for David. He is a real gent and he taught me something good – that it costs nothing to say 'Hello'.

I can say now that these two experiences certainly made me determined that if, or when, I reached the top and anyone ever asked me for an autograph, or a piece of my time, I will try to give them my time with good grace and respect. That is why I work hard to look after my many fans. I appreciate that's not always going to be easy or possible, but that's what I aim to achieve.

Actually, it was not until Formula Three that I realized that I had fans, people that admired me for what I did. When they wanted to come over and talk to me, it was just a pleasure for me. All of them were polite to me, and I was no one as far as I was concerned, but they were always there supporting me. I was not used to that, but I learned from it. I have got some great fans all over the world, including those who come all the way from Japan, just for a weekend, to watch me race! I always try to make time for them because from past experiences I know how important it is to make time for others.

When I got to GP2, I noticed that my time was getting more precious – but I made sure I had enough of it to go around and say thank you to everyone. When I reached Formula One, it got more and more difficult, but I knew to expect this, so when I went to my first Grand Prix, in Australia, I said to myself that I must make time for the fans. I worked out that if I planned to get to the track at eight, and that I had a meeting starting at half past eight, then there was not enough time, in that half an hour, to start signing autographs. So I said to myself, 'I'll get there at 7.30 and use that extra time to sign autographs.' What a great feeling it was to make others happy; that's a bit more energy in my energy bank. But I remember one day at Albert Park when I was just trying to juggle all the different events that were going on – I had a tyres briefing, an engineering meeting, and several other meetings and then I had to rush back to the hotel to do a HUGO BOSS and a Mercedes-Benz event, or something – and I was panicking. It all got to me. I didn't know how to judge it. I didn't have time to do autographs at the exit gate, where everyone was waiting outside the paddock, and I just walked on, and I kept walking. It was not a good feeling ignoring the fans, doing the one thing I promised I would never do. That was one of the single most distressing experiences I have ever had and it played on my mind all night.

So, next day, I made sure that I got a load of photos and posters and I signed about a hundred posters or more. I put 'Sorry' or 'Thank you' or something like that on them, and then

the following day I went in early and signed a load of autographs as well and gave each person a poster. It felt good – I
got all my energy back. A lot of fans who get the opportunity
to come up close are sometimes physically shaking with
nerves and I remember feeling it was incredible that I could
make anyone feel that way. I'm only human. I'm not this big
superstar that you see on TV. I am nothing special. I might be
a Formula One racing driver, but that does not make me any
different. As far as I am concerned we are all on the same
level. I want to take time out of my schedule to sign an autograph if it is going to make someone's day. Making people
happy is what makes me happy.

I do not believe in doing anything wrong to succeed.
Never. In my family we are all competitive and nobody likes to
lose. I would say my dad's the worst. He taught me how to win
and lose but even he would admit that losing is not a nice
experience to deal with – it does make your desire to succeed
even stronger, though I can see how difficult he finds it some
times. It shows in his face, of course, even after a game of pool
at home. And I can see it sometimes after races. We are alike,
too, in that we stick to the same way of doing things. As I said
earlier, we believe in the basics – honesty, loyalty and trust –
and that is why we all found the politics in Formula One this
year so hard to handle. As I said at the time, politics sucks.
Everyone knows about the controversy with Ferrari and, well,
the last thing any of us wanted was to be landed in something
like that in the middle of my rookie season.

I suppose it is to do with honesty that I want to do things properly . . . in an open way. I compete to win, but I always do my best and try to do things the right way. Maybe I am sometimes very highly charged and very determined, but I would never ever cheat to win. Never at all. That is why we all felt so much emotion when there were so many allegations being made against the team, against Vodafone McLaren Mercedes, this year. It was wrong. I never once believed any of the rumours or stories and I had complete belief in Ron Dennis and the team and the values they stand by.

In my own way, the only thing to do was to rise above it all, concentrate on the racing, continue to do my best and, most important of all, keep a smile on my face which, with everything kicking off, had been difficult. All my lessons in life, my dad's and my family's advice and encouragement and examples of how to live and how to behave, have stood me in good stead. When you have been through some of the stuff I went through as a kid, and when you have seen life through a really normal pair of eyes in Stevenage, in London, in Grenada and other places – all of that on top of my racing career gave me the right kind of grounding to cope with it. So I just did my thing.

Being able to control yourself, redeem yourself, is important. When I play computer games with Nic I always try my best to beat him. I never let him win. I never let anyone win at anything, at home or anywhere. I am always the same. I am just that competitive. I have to win at everything, but I would never cheat. I just love knowing that I won fair and square or that I tried my best.

Mental strength is so important. On the surface, it may look like I am pretty cool most of the time, but underneath I am a very emotional person. That is why these things matter. I love being at home with my family and the equilibrium that gives me. We are all emotional people in my family – that is part of our nature – but in this business, in Formula One, you have to be a bit cold and a bit selfish. I suppose we are all a bit selfish in our own lives and that comes out sometimes in all of us. But I find I can balance it all if I am around my family.

Racing takes up most of my weekends, so any weekends I do have off are so important and valuable to me, and, going back to square one, returning to my own home and occasionally going to my parents' house, the power station – that is important, too. It is where I do all my mental preparation and feel good. My strength is in the family, wherever we all are, as long as we are together.

There are loads of places where you can get mental strength and energy, but again there are loads of places you can lose energy! For me, the problems are energy wasters. And it is my dad's job to make sure that he helps me with that – he absorbs all of the negative energy when it happens. It is too easy to be sucked into things and just find you are drained by it all.

This whole thing about changing negative energy into positive energy is not rocket science. It is just about trying to look on the positive side and turn this or that mistake, or whatever, into something positive. I cannot do it with everything. Sometimes it is just too big to put through my small generator. So, that is when my dad absorbs it; or I put it onto someone else – I might call my mum, or a best friend, telling him about the problem – and then it's their problem! As long as I keep the same set of principles, I will be fine.

I have been racing since I was eight years old and I have learned what works for me. I always try to remember to appreciate the opportunity I've been given and I always give 100 per cent. I always say, 'Keep your family as close as possible.' These are the things I believe in and they have done me well.

In my career, it is the same. McLaren and Mercedes-Benz have been incredibly loyal to us and, hopefully, we will be loyal to them and I'll see out most of my career with them. For me, loyalty matters. In terms of friendship, it means being someone others can trust. And that works both ways. I am the sort of person who tells it all and can be quite blunt. Sometimes I do not realize that I may have affected someone, for worse or better, but it is just me being honest.

I know I am a lucky person. I have a good life, I have been given a talent and I have enjoyed myself very much, for most of the time, in my twenty-two years. It is never easy though. No way. Not for me, not for my dad and not for my family. We have had some extremely hard times and some extremely good times. But – and I think this is the most important thing – we have learned from them all.

CHAPTER

CONFIDENCE

'My racing career may not have started properly until I was eight, but it had in fact been part of my life much earlier. As a teenager, sadly my enthusiasm was not shared by all and my career nearly ended before it had started because of a case of mistaken identity by my school.'

MY START IN LIFE WAS PRETTY NORMAL. I was born at the Lister Hospital in Stevenage, Hertfordshire, on 7 January 1985. I was named Lewis Carl Davidson Hamilton. My dad's middle name is Carl and Nic also has Carl as a middle name. The name Lewis was just a name that my parents liked at the time. The name Davidson is taken from my granddad

Stevenage was one of the 'new towns' built after the Second World War and is a typical commuter town with both local and international business facilities and good rail and road links to London, in the south, and to the north of England. Thousands of people travel from Stevenage to London and back every day on the train and my dad was one of them. He worked for British Rail while my mum worked in the local council offices. My mum and dad lived in a council house in Peartree Way, on the Shephall Estate, in Stevenage. My mum had two daughters

– Samantha and Nicola – from a previous relationship before she met my dad. Sammy and Nicky were about two and three when my dad came into their lives. It was not a luxurious or a privileged neighbourhood, but it was also not as bad as some.

My first school was just down the end of our road, the Peartree Spring Nursery School. My second primary school, Peartree Infant and Junior School, was a five-minute walk around the corner. For my secondary school I chose the John Henry Newman School, a Roman Catholic secondary, before completing my education at the Cambridge Arts and Sciences College. I have to say it was not as straightforward as it sounds, and there were a few ups and downs along the way. My interest in karting and motor racing, which took me away a lot at weekends as I grew older, did not always fit in with the strict thinking of some people. At school, I used to keep my interest in racing to myself.

My racing career may not have started properly until I was eight, but it had in fact been part of my life much earlier. As a teenager, sadly my enthusiasm was not shared by all and my career nearly ended before it had started because of a case of mistaken identity by my school.

To this day, I find it difficult to talk about this because it nearly destroyed my faith in the education system. But I think it's important to set the record straight on a few things in my life that have been reported inaccurately in the last year or so. I wish it could be forgotten forever but some things just need to be said.

It was 2001, I was sixteen and a few important months away from sitting my GCSEs at John Henry Newman School. In January of that year there was a serious incident at the school involving a pupil who was attacked in the school toilets by a gang of about six boys. I was accused of kicking the pupil. This was not true. I, like many others, had been hanging around waiting for the next lesson to start and had entered the toilets around the time that the attack was taking place. I was not involved in the attack but knew the boys involved.

The headteacher thought differently and wrote a letter to my parents advising them that I was excluded from school along with six other pupils and stating the reasons why. I couldn't believe it. I was so upset. I didn't know how I was going to explain it to my parents. I walked around in a daze, not really knowing where I was going for a while, I even considered running away and then eventually I went home. When I gave the letter to my dad and step-mum Linda they were obviously extremely disappointed and really mad – not so much with me but with the headteacher – although I remember my dad said to me, 'Congratulations, you've done something that I never managed to do!' I knew that I had done nothing wrong so this made it all the worse.

We decided to go back to the school. I went with Linda and my mum to speak to the headteacher. When they arrived at the school, the headteacher was not sympathetic to anything they said to him and he maintained that I had kicked the pupil and that I was correctly excluded. I knew I was innocent but he did not appear to be interested. Subsequent letters to the local education authority, our local MP, the Education Secretary and even the Prime Minister, were of no help. No one appeared to listen – no one either wanted to or had the time. We were on our own and I was out of school.

I found it very frustrating and upsetting, with everyone seemingly against me except my family, some true friends, and McLaren and Mercedes-Benz. I could not understand how I found myself in such an awful situation.

We launched an appeal to the Governors' Discipline Committee of the school, but the appeal failed. We then appealed to the Local Education Authority where the matter was considered by the Exclusion Appeal Panel.

From the very beginning I told my dad that I was innocent and he did everything he could to prove this. It was just typical of my dad: when something is wrong he will go to the ends of the earth to find out the truth.

Anyway, it took weeks to resolve (although it seemed so much longer at the time) with documents going backwards and forwards. I was still out of school and having private tuition paid for by my family until our appeal could be heard. My dad had gone through the evidence and meticulously studied all the documents and witness statements and he thought he had a pretty good case prepared.

At the hearing, the Exclusion Appeal Panel concluded (after a thorough investigation including hearing oral evidence from witnesses) that my appeal should be upheld and that I should be fully reinstated to school. The panel concluded that I was not guilty of kicking the pupil. They also found that in fact there had been a serious case of mistaken identity, or, as they put it, 'unfortunate confusion' with another pupil who was said to be one of the individuals involved.

While the matter should have been resolved at that stage (the beginning of April 2001), the battle was not over as the school refused to reinstate me back to my class. It was the same for some other pupils who had successfully appealed. Instead, I was offered segregated tuition. All this was going on just before I took my GCSEs, so it was really bad timing. My dad arranged for alternative private tuition and exams. In the end I sat the GCSEs in different locations. It was not ideal as I had missed crucial weeks of education but I did my best given the circumstances. Some exams I sat back at the school, but they wouldn't let me go back to my class so I had to sit on my own. The rest I sat at other local schools.

I didn't enjoy school that much anyway before the incident, except for my friends and the sports, of course, but when this happened I thought that everything I had worked for was going down the drain. I was worried, too, that I would lose my racing career and opportunity with McLaren because Ron Dennis, just like my dad, had always told me, 'Lewis, you've got to work hard at school.' Well, I wasn't the perfect student, but I did the best I could and did what I had to in order to get by.

Following this bad experience, and the unnecessary stresses and strains brought upon my whole family, my dad decided it was time that we moved away from Stevenage. We relocated fifteen minutes away to a lovely quiet village where no one knew us at the time. When I look back, I think what a shame it was that the end of my Stevenage school years was spoiled for me. Although the Local Education Authority has admitted it was all a mistake, neither I nor my family have received an apology, private or public. It is much too late for me now but it would be good for me to know that something like this could never happen to another pupil. One thing is for sure: without my dad's attention to detail I would have been lost. It has given me a completely different perspective on school life.

After that I was glad to eventually leave John Henry Newman School. I moved to the Cambridge Arts and Sciences College. CATS, as it is known, was a fantastic place. The teachers were professional and the pupils too. I got the train most times until I passed my driving test and then I would drive there. It was a really good experience. I had the opportunity to stay at the College, but I did not want to share dorms with people who I did not even know and I thought I would miss my family. To be honest, looking back now, I should have boarded because it would have been good to live on my own and to spend time with people of my own age who were not from the motor racing world.

There were people of all backgrounds: wealthy kids and not-so-wealthy ones. It was a real mixed bunch. It was a pleasurable experience for me. The staff were really nice: they spoke to you on the level and not as if they were above you. I also felt more fulfilled and began to value myself differently. I was happier. I liked design, technology and music, but my dad wasn't keen on me taking music and recommended that I do business studies. He thought that it would be more useful and relevant in motor racing and that it would give me a better chance at a decent job should I ever need it to fall back on.

I didn't think business studies was right for me which is probably the reason I didn't do so well in the exam. I was not even slightly interested and if you're forced to do something you don't like, you're not going to do as well in it. I was into music. I played the guitar and I also wanted to learn the drums. I always wanted to be like Phil Collins – he can play everything: guitar, drums, piano, bass guitar . . . Music was something I enjoyed and wanted to do at college, but in the end I listened to my dad. I still didn't like business studies and, for that matter, some other subjects as well.

But I really enjoyed CATS and the city of Cambridge itself. Before I went there, I just thought, 'I'm going to be a bum!' I never said to myself, 'I'm going to be a professional racing driver' or anything like that. It did not cross my mind. Once I went to college, I realized that I could enjoy more things and I bucked up my ideas a lot. I felt like I really wanted to do well. Something clicked for me. It was a much smaller class and I got on well with my teachers. Bar a couple of really smart girls and maybe one smart lad, I was one of the top students in my class. I was even learning and understanding my science studies! But I am the kind of person who wants to be able to do everything. Aside from music, I particularly wanted to do French. It turned out to be my best subject. I almost aced French.

I spent some of my teenage years kart racing in France and Italy and so found it relatively easy to speak French with a French accent and Italian with an Italian accent. I speak more confidently in Italian than in French, I don't know why. But when I go to France it all comes back to me. I want to be able to really speak it fluently, although I can't comprehend it well. I don't know how anyone can! How can they store all that information? Then again, I don't really speak good enough English, let alone another language . . .

It got tough for me as time went by, though. My college days were Tuesday, Wednesday and Thursday and I had to work hard to catch up on the work I missed, because the Formula Renault single-seater testing always took place on the same days. So I took extra lessons, just as I had done when I was at secondary school when we had a tutor to help me. I had to get there an hour earlier or work later. I worked some really long days to make sure I caught up. It was the first time in my life in my academic work that I actually thought to myself, 'I can do this and I can do well in exams.'

When I went to CATS, they were willing to give me time. They were totally open to my racing. They didn't even ask about it. They were just . . . 'This is what you have to do, if that's what you want to do then go and do it . . .' They never said,

'Oh, Lewis, you shouldn't be taking this time off.' They never questioned it. Instead it was, 'Well, how can we work around it?' And that's why it was so good. They worked with me.

In fairness there were also some good memories from my Stevenage schooldays. I was reminded of them when Ashley Young, now a very successful professional footballer, was picked to play for England. We were in the same year and we used to play together in the school football team. From what I remember of Ashley, he was a very good football player and a nice guy.

I really liked playing football. I started in midfield and I would go into a tackle and go in so hard that I risked breaking my leg. I did not deliberately foul people, or go in with studs showing or anything like that, but I would give it a real sliding tackle and if I got the ball I would go charging off and do the best job I could with it. My problem was that I always kept my head down. I was always looking at the ball instead of where I was going and so would end up being tackled or run into another player. I always thought I did twice the amount of work of any other player on the field but for half the result! But I knew, at least, that I did the best job I could.

In general, I liked competitive sports – I didn't want to read about the rules or go and watch it; I just wanted to do it because it was good fun – but motor racing was different. I read, studied and knew all the rules.

I was relatively good at most sports: I played for the cricket team, the basketball team, the footy team. I was on the athletics team and I did javelin, discus and the 800 metres and won the occasional event on school sports days.

Nic also loves competitive sports but is unable to compete in most. Still, he tries and he tries and he never gets down or depressed about things. If he fell over, he would get straight back up and get on with it even if he was in pain. He made such a big impact on me and on the way I think about things. Nic is blessed in so many ways.

Even now, I am sometimes quite hard on Nic about small things, I just want to help him learn and not to take anything for granted. Most importantly, I want him to do well, even better than me, in his education and exams and so I keep on top of him about this. He always tells me I am the best and he never really talks to me about my driving. He is so sensible.

CHAPTER  4

STARTING OUT

'My dad would always stand on the inside of the circuit at the hairpin. He watched to see where the best drivers were braking … "You've got to brake here, at least a metre later than the other competitors."'

MY DAD HAS ALWAYS BEEN MY MANAGER and my adviser. I remember years ago, when I was about twelve, in Junior Yamaha and at a race track giving an interview. I said, 'My dad gives me advice on what to do on the track, but I don't listen to it because he doesn't know what it's like out there.'

I regret saying that because it's not true. I remember I was angry at the time because things were not going so well. Dad's got a much wiser head on his shoulders than me so he knows a lot of the stuff he says is true. He's always right. It got to the point where I took bits out of what he was saying and then added my own bit – what I thought should be right. I think that's why we work well as a team. We gel together.

At a young age, he was very hard on me and now that I am older and a little bit wiser I fully understand and appreciate why. I can probably guarantee that he was harder on me than any other driver's father was on his son. I don't just mean in life at the track – I mean in life generally. He brought me up to appreciate people and to appreciate general values: you know, be polite and always say thank you, always have a smile on your face, do not be rude – all those things. If I made a mistake in that sort of area, where I wasn't polite, I was made aware of it. I'm easy to get on with. I'm just as normal as any other driver, or any other person. When I started karting, my dad did a kind of deal with me. He said that he would support me going racing, but only if I worked harder at school. I remember my dad had to work three jobs just to make ends meet and to keep his end of the bargain. During the day he worked for British Rail – as it was back then – as a computer manager, having risen through the ranks over 14 years from an admin clerk. When he arrived back home he would go straight out again and erect 'For Sale' sign boards in his suit for a local estate agent. I think he only used to get 50 pence a board but it all helped and every penny counted. In any other spare time, my dad used to knock on doors trying to book double-glazing appointments for his friend Terry Holland's business. It was not a job he enjoyed but he still did it.

The first time I sat in a go-kart was when we all went on holiday to Ibiza. It was in August 1988, and I was three years old. I had not really been anywhere abroad before then for a summer holiday, so I remember it pretty well. Both my dad and Linda were working for British Rail and they were located at King's Cross. I remember they were living in a small one-bedroom flat in Hatfield. We stayed in a mobile home camp in Ibiza and we travelled one way by plane and one way by train as this was all they could afford. The plane journey was something they saved up for, while the train tickets were part of a concession through working for the railway. A big group of us went on that holiday. The real highlight for me in Ibiza was the trip to the kart track.

They had little electric kiddie karts and the track was very small. It was less than a hundred metres long, probably only about sixty metres, but I loved it. I got in a kart and straightaway I knew I was going to enjoy it. I remember thinking I was Ayrton Senna, it just felt natural.

After that, nobody gave it a second thought. My dad was just a railway worker and I was just a kid. We went home and I thought that was it, but my dad remembered how much we had all enjoyed it, especially me. We thought nothing of it until a couple of years later.

For my fifth birthday I got my first remote control car. I remember them putting the batteries in this little car. I drove it up and down the hallway and tried it outside, too. I really liked it. I suppose that was the beginning, or at least the beginning of the beginning. I was consciously hooked on cars from that point.

A few months later my dad brought me an even bigger and better 1/12th scale electric remote control car and spent days building it up from all the bits in a box when he came home from work. I loved it. I was always pestering him to keep recharging the batteries. Eventually my dad thought enough's enough, if we are going to muck around with this car then let's do it properly and join a club. So we did just that. We went down to our local model shop Models in Motion, in the Old Town in Stevenage, and we joined the racing club and went remote control car racing every weekend on Sunday mornings. It was great fun for us both. There were like fifty adults racing and just two kids – and one of them was me. I found I was really competitive. My dad loved it and pretty soon he was helping me with everything. I guess that is when he became my first mechanic.

We used to go to the shop and get all kinds of new parts, and paint, and try to improve the car. We went racing at a village called Bennington with my electric remote control car packed in the back of Linda's car – a white Mini Metro that cost my dad £100. In my first year I came second in the club championship, having beaten the adult who had been racing for years. They were a great bunch of people from what I remember and the camaraderie was brilliant. They didn't mind me, a little kid, joining in their fun and beating them at it. It was through the hobby shop Models in Motion that I got my chance to go on BBC television's *Blue Peter*. I was just six years old. At the end of my first season the club gave me a special award for the most impressive driver – so with this and ending up on television, what more could a kid ask for!

The next step came when we moved up from electric remote control cars to a 1/8th scale petrol-engined car called a

Turbo Burns. I still have the car to this day. I remember it cost my dad a whopping £250 to buy second hand from someone at the track. I was still living in Peartree Way then, with my mum, but my dad and Linda had by that time moved to Shear-water Close in Stevenage where they bought a small three-bedroomed house with its own garden. It was our house. It was when Linda was expecting Nic, so they needed more space. Dad bought the house in Shearwater Close and let the flat in Hatfield. He couldn't really afford to keep either but somehow he just managed because he had to. It meant we were now living in Stevenage closer to my mum and that was good for me. Nic was born the following year, in March 1992, and that summer, when I was seven, I went to Rye House at Hoddesdon, in Hertfordshire, for my first ride in a real go-kart on a real kart track. My dad took me for a day out following what we thought was a successful year in remote control car racing. We knew absolutely nothing about kart racing but we were just having fun. I went out on the little circuit at the back of Rye House – I mean the little one that no one else would dare go on – and I had a really good time. I got the bug for karting from that moment. That was it, that was all I ever wanted to do. It was wicked and my dad was now in trouble!

A few weeks later, there were some pretty strange goings-on in the shed at the back of our house. My dad used to sit most nights in the shed preparing my remote control cars, a job he had done for nearly eighteen months, when suddenly he built this extension to the shed from wood that he bought down the local DIY shop. The shed door used to be located on the side of the shed but now it was transformed into a pair of front double doors. I got my first go-kart that Christmas. I remember I was at my mum's for the morning on that Christmas Day and then I went to my dad's house. My mum was just dropping me off and my dad wasn't in. I looked through the letter box and I could see down the hallway and onto the table. And there, I saw something really big in wrapping paper. I guess I ruined the surprise. I remember I was walking backwards into the house trying to act like I hadn't even noticed this big monster of a present on the table! Eventually, I got to open it after my dad strung it out and pretended it wasn't for me. You know what: they had given me the best gift that I'd ever had in my life up to that point.

They had also bought me a pale blue driving suit and matching race gloves, and a red FM helmet. I had the biggest smile ever on my face. We went out and I drove it on the street. We lived in a quiet close so it was okay, plus it was Christmas Day so why not? It turned out that this kart was a tenth-hand, rickety old thing when dad bought it, but he worked night and day to rebuild it in his purpose-built extended shed. He did everything to make it as good as new: completely re-sprayed it and polished everything that could be polished. That way, I would fit in with all the other kids whose parents could afford brand new presents. I was truly thrilled. I was buzzing. Of course, I wanted to try it out properly and, on my birthday two weeks later, we took it down to Rye House in the back of my dad's Vauxhall Cavalier, with boot open, kart hanging out – what a sight we were – but we didn't care; we were going karting. I had my first run on Saturday, 9 January, two days after my birthday. I was eight years old. And the rest is history!

Seriously, it was a real big thing in my life. It was when I started my karting career. I began racing at the then Hoddesdon Kart Racing Club, Rye House which was run by Alan Kilby and Harry Sowden. I raced in the Cadet Populars class as a novice and was instantly on the pace. If you are a new driver, you have to wear black plates for your first six races so that all the other drivers know you are a novice. Over a number of weekends, I brought home six first-place novice trophies from various circuits.

I was now ready and qualified to go on to yellow plates and start racing with the bigger, more experienced, drivers. I took part in my first 'yellow plate' race on 2 May 1993, I think at Clay Pigeon Kart Club down in Dorset, and I won against all the odds.

In my first year of cadet karting I was quite often quicker than some of the older and more experienced kids and occasionally if I overtook them on the circuit they would come up to me off the track and warn me off. It happened to my dad also, their dads would warn my dad off. I was already learning karate and so my dad decided to take it up as well, as we thought maybe this karting stuff is a bit more physical than we first thought. We both joined the local Stevenage Shotokan

Karate Club run by Mike Nursey, a 6th Dan. I managed to get up to one grade short of intermediate black belt when I was ten. A lot of people have said I am black belt and I have not really corrected them as it has been easier to just say nothing. Although I was smaller for my age than most of my competitors, I was never scared to stand up for myself. My dad reached the same grade but we were away so much with karting that it was impossible to compete for our black belts.

We would go testing at Rye House occasionally during the week but mostly every weekend. My dad would always stand on the inside of the circuit at the hairpin. He watched to see where the best drivers were braking and he would go and stand there and say to me, 'You've got to brake here, at least a metre later than the other competitors.' Then, he would move a metre further and say, 'You've got to brake here!' So I had to brake later than the drivers who were braking late and doing well. And that's how, and where, I learned how to brake late. I was pushing and pushing, and lots of the time I went off because it was just impossible to brake that late. And he would say, 'No, you can do it, go on, you can do it.' Eventually, it worked and I could brake later than any of my competitors and still keep the momentum in the kart. This was one of the keys to my success on the karting circuits.

I also had my first crash at Rye House on a practice day. I think it was Saturday, 30 January, the day before my first 'black plate' race day. It was getting close to the circuit closing time and we were just about to finish. We were on our last

‘ Fun on three wheels during a holiday... ’

My first run in a kiddie-kart during a family holiday in Ibiza in August 1988, aged three.

Right An early photoshoot…

Far right My brother Nic's third birthday party.

Happy with another grade and certificate in karate.

My first kart, aged eight.

Right Preparing for my first race in my new kart and helmet.

Below Champions of the Future – a cadet race winner.

Left Me with Ron Dennis, at the Belgian Grand Prix in 1996.

Right Kart Masters – and another win!

Meeting Murray Walker at the Autosport Awards 1995.

Above Team MBM – alongside fellow racer Nico Rosberg in 2001.

Right Formula Renault with Nic in 2001.

Below Becoming 2000 Formula A European Champion.

Above My dad has always been my manager and mentor – and also my chief mechanic when karts needed fixing.

Above Prince Charles came to the McLaren factory at Woking where we swapped a few tips on racing.

Below and inset You win some, you lose some – it can be a lonely place sometimes.

‘ **Meeting David Couthard at the McLaren Mercedes Young Driver Support Programme in 1998.** ’

Posing for the camera in the old McLaren trophy room.

Dreaming and hoping that one day…

Spending time playing pool with Nic.

Playing the guitar, and music in general, is
one of my favourite ways of chilling out
and relaxing.

couple of runs and some dude came up on the inside of me and clipped me into the first corner. I didn't even know he was there and he sent me off flat-out into the tyre wall. I went straight into the tyres – my kart was all bent and damaged and I had a bleeding nose. My dad charged up from the bottom end of the circuit fearing that I had hurt myself, but when he got to me the first thing I said was, 'Can you fix it for tomorrow?' I wasn't bothered at all about me. I was just in a bit of a daze. My dad drove all the way to the other side of London to find the parts for my Allkart. Eventually he got the necessary parts from a nice man called Bruno Ferrari. Bruno used to tune race engines for Dan Wheldon and a few others at the time. Dan was then a huge karting star even though he was only about thirteen. Anyway, my dad got the parts and fixed my kart; we went racing the next day and I brought home my first trophy!

Eventually I competed in events all over the country nearly every two weeks. I remember going up to Larkhall, in Scotland, and staying in this weird hotel where everything was painted black. It was a real scary Addams Family type of place! And there was a place called Rowrah up in the Lake District way up north, where it seemed to rain non-stop. But it was all good experience, travelling out into the middle of nowhere just to race karts. The whole family used to go along in my dad's red Vauxhall Cavalier with a little old box trailer that danced around all over the place behind us. We stuck all the gear in this little box thing, then we put the go-kart on top of it, with all these different straps to stop the thing from flying away. And off we'd go.

When I was nine, I entered my first British Cadet Kart Championship. We had sold our old Allkart and bought a new bright green Zip Kart made by Martin Hines. Martin owned the company and was a very successful figure in the karting business and he ran a team called the Zip Young Guns. We couldn't afford to be in the Zip Young Guns team and so remained independent but with advice, help and assistance from Martin.

Eventually, we bought a larger second-hand box trailer with a roller door on the back, which was a huge improvement. But then the poor old Cavalier had to drag this heavy trailer around all the time. I remember we would travel up to Larkhall in the wind and the rain, and when we arrived most of the other competitors had camper vans or caravans, while we had a box trailer. Linda would have to bring the microwave and kettle from the kitchen and sit in the back of the box trailer during the cold and windy days with Nic, then aged two, on her lap. That was hard on everyone but they did it for me and we thoroughly enjoyed every minute of it.

By this time, my dad had even got a Calor gas heater and put it at the back of the trailer. So Linda and Nic were in the back, jackets on, freezing cold, and then there was me and my dad, at the front of the trailer trying to prepare the kart. I remember Linda always brought a red flask along, full of chicken noodle soup.

After that weekend, my dad said 'never again' and somehow worked a few more jobs to buy a really old Bedford camper van that Linda named 'Maureen'. Life started to get better. No more cold, damp soggy baps but instead we had toast in the mornings before a race – heaven!

It is hard for any family who have to find the money to race, particularly so in the case of my parents who just had normal day jobs. For those first three or four years, before we had backing from McLaren, it was probably a lot more of a strain for my family than it was for me, and especially for my dad. For me, it was just get in the camper, go to the racetrack, sign on, do my driver's briefing and then go and race – and that felt natural. We didn't always win; it was tough and I'd get grumpy like a spoilt kid. I just did not like to lose – and neither did my dad.

From these early days my dad has been my manager, with Linda in full support. It has really been a family team, Nic included. Occasionally our relationship has been strained by the pressures of motor racing but that is just normal. My dad has been the motivator and the strength that keeps us all going. To be father and manager can be tricky; it is not easy balancing both of those roles. Sometimes, I know I can be very cold and just treat him as a manager, but then I love him to bits for what he is and what he's done for me – and he's my dad! It's not straightforward. You wake up and he's the first, or second, person you see and so you've got that natural bond. Then you remember he is your manager too. But it works for us. And my dad, and my family, have made more sacrifices than you would believe.

I have proved him wrong at some points in my life, but, like I said, he is almost always right. Even though he is not the driver experiencing what I am experiencing, he is just as involved as me, if not more. He is just trying to do his best. It is a very strange relationship we have because he is so driven. He is so committed but never ever pushy. I said I wanted to race karts and he said, 'Okay, if we are going to do it, then we are going to do it properly or not at all' and that was it. It was either everything or nothing and that is still where I am today.

My step-mum, Linda, is fantastic. I was so young when my dad met Linda that I did not understand what had gone on between my parents. It tells you something about a person when they are prepared to take on the responsibility of looking after someone else's kid: me. Ninety per cent of the people I know that have divorced parents and step-parents have a tough time because one does not like the other. Linda is Nic's mum and what I love about her is the fact that she had Nic, her real son, but never ever treated us differently. My dad could not have picked a better step-mum for me. As I said earlier, Linda is the best step-mum in the world.

I honestly do not think I would be where I am today if my parents and step-parents had not worked hard together. With my brother, as we grow up, the bond is getting stronger and stronger. For me, it's the most valuable thing I have in my life. My dad has been the main driving force for me. The way I am now is down to him. A lot of my friends did not have their fathers around and mine was there for me. So, respect to him for that. He has certain morals and there are a lot of important values that he has taught me. I know some people say he is overprotective, but he has always been committed to making sure that I maximize my opportunities to have a better life than he had. Dad is the one who started it all when I was just a boy. Without him, I do not think any of this would have happened at all.

CHAPTER 5

CLIMBING

'There was a point where I asked myself, "Am I going to be able to do this?" I remember sitting with my dad in the car telling him that I wanted to stop ... he just said, "Yeah, okay, we'll just stop." He didn't really mean it, but I was doubting myself, not feeling that I was the man at all.'

I REMEMBER IT SO CLEARLY: me on the passenger seat of this old camper van and my dad driving, the two of us singing together: *'We are the champions, we are the champions'* . . . At the end, the song goes *'of the world'* but we sang *'of England'*, or *'of Britain'*, or something like that. It was a great day. And it was just the start . . .

In the early karting years, when I was between eight and twelve years of age, it was all great fun – the travelling, the competitions, meeting different people in different places and just generally having good family time together – but it started to get pretty serious when I won my first British Cadet Kart Championship in 1995 at the age of ten.

The year before, I'd experienced the real dangers of motor racing for the first time. I remember it was early May and I was at Rye House. I had just finished a race and my dad, quietly, came over to me and said, 'Lewis, Ayrton Senna's just died . . . He's had a terrible crash at Imola . . .' I remember how I did not want to show emotion in front of my dad because I thought he would have a go at me and so I walked round the back, where no one was looking, and I just cried. I really struggled the rest of that day. I could not stop imagining what had gone on. I was only nine years old. The man who inspired me was dead. He was a superhero, you know, and that was him . . . just gone.

In 1996 I won the McLaren Mercedes Cadet Champions of the Future Series and the Sky TV Masters title. After that, we moved up into Junior Yamaha in 1997. There was a lot of talk about which was the best standard and category to be in. We chose Junior Yamaha because we thought it was a better career path than Junior TKM, the rival series. People would say we were avoiding TKM because it had fiercer competition but we knew where we were headed and what we wanted to learn from our racing and it wasn't to be found in Junior TKM, although it was also a great series.

That year I won both the McLaren Mercedes Junior Yamaha Champion of the Future series and the British Super One Junior Yamaha Kart Championship with a round to spare. That was also the year when I was invited, by Ron Dennis, to go to Belgium, to the Grand Prix at Spa-Francorchamps as part of the prize for winning the championship.

In 1998, I was invited to be a part of the McLaren Mercedes Young Driver Support Programme. This was a golden opportunity to be supported by a major Formula One team and car manufacturer. My dad was delighted. As I have said, we were not exactly rolling in cash and, although we were getting by, the McLaren contract certainly provided us with the financial comfort that all young budding racing drivers desired.

I also raced in Europe for the first time, helped by the recommendation of Martin Hines to the Italian Top Kart manufacturer and racing team. I had my first European race in Belgium and it was not a great race, but it was just good showing up. I impressed the people from Top Kart and we got another chance to race for them, in Italy. I did my first race in Parma and in the same race was this kid called Nico Rosberg, now a Formula One driver with Williams. I remember we had this awesome race where I was behind him, both of us miles in front of the other guys. I just sat on his tail the whole race, played it cool, and then on the last lap I overtook him on a straight and won the race. That was the day Nico's father, Keke Rosberg, the 1982 Formula One World Champion, came up to me and said, 'That was an awesome race, well done' and that's when my relationship with Nico started. From then on, we became best friends, hanging around with each other all the time throughout our teenage karting years.

A few months later we went to Hockenheim for the German Grand Prix. Keke, Nico and I sat down with Ron Dennis. He said to us, 'I'm planning to put together a team. Are you two going to be able to stay friends if we have this team and you're competing against each other?' We said 'Yes' without hesitation and Keke created our own kart team called Team

MBM. We never really found out what the MBM stood for but I assumed it meant Mercedes-Benz McLaren. We raced together in 2000 and had a fantastic year winning nearly every major race in our class. That was one of the most amazing years of my career: I won the European Championship and the World Cup in Japan. I especially remember one weekend, in the European Championship, at a place called Val d'Argenton in France, for very special reasons.

The week before, I had fallen off my bike and hurt my wrist. I tried to hide the swelling because I was really worried about what my dad would say but the pain was so bad I eventually had to tell him what had happened. My dad called Ron Dennis and asked for his help. Ron called the then Formula One doctor Professor Sid Watkins and a friend who put my wrist in a special cast. So, we travelled over to France and took part in the race weekend. I won my first two heats, then suddenly someone complained to the Clerk of the Course about my plaster cast. The next thing I knew, I was excluded from the event. Naturally, with the European Championship at stake, my dad pleaded with whoever would listen but eventually he contacted Ron to explain what had happened. Ron was actually at the Austrian Grand Prix but he spoke with a Senior Member of the FIA who intervened and I was reinstated. I missed one of my heats and therefore started lower on the grid for the first final but still managed to win both feature races, the second one ahead of Robert Kubica, who is now racing for BMW in Formula One.

I had a bad year in karts in 2001 when Nico and I thought we would move up to the final karting class – Formula Super A as it was then – and try to win the championship. It didn't go well at all. We were developing our own chassis with Dino Cheisa our Team MBM manager and it was tough but it was something we wanted to do for Dino and his team. It was a good learning experience.

At the end of the year we went to single-seaters. McLaren arranged for me to have a test with Manor Motorsport in their Formula Renault car. It was always going to be tricky, never having been in a racing car before, and I crashed after about three laps, taking out the right rear corner of the car. It did not put them off too much though, and after they fixed the car I got straight back in and did okay. I started my first year of the British Formula Renault series in 2001 with Manor Motorsport. Moving on from my fantastic years in karting to single-seater racing was something I had been looking forward to for some time. I had my first race at Donington Park in November. I had qualified fifth. I remember all these cars shooting past me at the start. It was like I had never raced before – well, I hadn't in cars. I couldn't believe just how different it was in cars as opposed to karts. In karting I was a king, but now in single-seaters I was back to basics. It was so aggressive on that first lap it was unreal, and I was like, 'Shoot, I'm going to have to pull my finger out!' It was not like karting, where you could just roll around the paddock and have some fun, get in the kart and drive. You had to be there paying attention to all the data, working with the engineers and all that stuff.

In 2002 I had quite tough times through the Formula Renault days and there were moments when I would come home and my dad was on at me for one thing or another. I was having problems keeping up at school, I was struggling. Actually, there was a point where I asked myself, 'Am I going to be able to do this?' I remember sitting with my dad in the car, telling him that I wanted to stop. My dad is very emotional about my racing and, being peed off, he just said, 'Yeah, okay, we'll just stop.' He didn't really mean it, but I was doubting myself, not feeling that I was the man at all. But things changed: from that low point in my life I got myself together, won some races and then came third in my first full year of Formula Renault.

The next year, 2003, I had a slow start before something just clicked, and then I just blew everyone away. I won ten races out of fifteen that season. I came second in two of them and third in one and because I had won the championship, I did not have to race the last two races. It was such a great year with Manor Motorsport's Formula Renault team that I decided I wanted to stay with Manor and move up into the British Formula Three series with them for a couple of end of season races. From the first time in the car I was quick and setting the pace but I had much to learn. Although my pace was good the races didn't quite finish as I expected. I had a huge shunt at Brands Hatch where I had the misfortune of being involved in someone else's accident but, that aside, I had a fantastic time.

For 2004, the team decided to move from the British Formula Three series to the Formula Three Euroseries with me as their driver. I did okay but it was the absolutely worst year of my racing career both because of the car and my relationship with the team. It was obviously difficult for the team as it was their first year in the championship and neither they nor I had ever raced on most of the European circuits before. It was a huge learning curve for us all, but I did feel that I was the one being blamed for poor results. It did cause quite a lot of tension between the team, me and my dad. In what I felt were very challenging circumstances, I won one race and finished fifth overall. This was a very frustrating period. Towards the end of that year, I had a really, really difficult time when we fell out of contract with McLaren. We were unhappy about the year we had just had and this was part of the reason that we had a disagreement over where I should race in 2005. I wanted to move on but McLaren recommended that I stay another year in Formula Three with Manor. This was not what I wanted. I had given it much thought over the previous few months and had also discussed it with my family and I eventually decided that I was prepared to give up my contract with McLaren rather than stay for another year. McLaren couldn't see it at the time and told me to go away at the end of 2004 and analyse my next move.

I had been at Manor Motorsport for three years and thought it was a good time to move on. I wanted to go somewhere else and learn from other people. I thought I could do that in GP2. McLaren disagreed. So we came out of contract.

My last two races of 2004 were to be in Macau and Bahrain and, as I was now without McLaren, I had to find my own sponsorship money to get there. I was going through a tough time with everything in my life. The team I had always wanted to be a part of had cancelled my contract because of a disagreement about the next step in my career. My dad and I then set about finding sponsorship money. My girlfriend at the time, Jodia, said, 'Hey, my dad owns this company in Hong Kong, and he would love to sponsor you.' I told her there was no way I wanted her to do that, but she went and sorted it out anyway. Basically, Jo's dad paid for my racing in Macau. It was a last attempt for me to make an impression in the world of Formula Three. So I went to Macau and won the first race with Jo's dad's company livery on my car but unfortunately crashed out on the second lap of the main race having started from pole position. It was one of the most disappointing races of my life. I thought the whole world had folded in on me and that was it – the end.

My dad was devastated because here we were with no McLaren Mercedes-Benz contract, no money, and no takers. The following weekend we were in Bahrain for the Formula Three Superprix, which was the last race of the year for Formula Three. The Manor Motorsport team actually funded this race which was much appreciated and pretty incredible considering the tough year we'd had until then and I remain grateful to all the guys at Manor Motorsport. In qualifying, I made a huge mistake. I ended up twenty-second on the grid after damaging my rear floor on the kerb. It was a really low point. My dad was unhappy that I had possibly just blown a great opportunity to shine after the disappointment of Macau. We were both devastated but my dad in particular because as usual he felt responsible for everything, the loss of McLaren, the situation we were in, and he was worried about where he would find the money to keep my career going and to fund the following year's racing. He was so depressed and worried that he booked an early flight home so that he could make better use of his time making calls and focusing on getting help. I know he was really feeling the pressure because I had no sponsor and at that stage not enough good performances to attract new ones. Before he left, he made sure I knew all about it, leaving me to kick myself for the rest of that day and all night.

I woke up in the morning with a fresh head and feeling more determined than ever. For the Sunday race, my dad had the team stick his company name on the side of the car. The company was called Hedge-Connect. Hedge-Connect was a disaster recovery business and it was incredibly appropriate as I eventually found out. I started the first race twenty-second on the grid and finished eleventh. In the second and main race, I started eleventh and finished first. I couldn't believe it – from nothing I had triumphed. It was awesome. Afterwards, I called my dad and he was stunned. No one could believe it – I had come from twenty-second in the first race to win in the main race. The racing magazines called it my 'Bahrain Transplant' and a transplant it certainly was. From a bad weekend in Macau to winning unexpectedly in Bahrain, everything had changed instantly, as it can do in motor racing. In karting, I had won from the back many times, but to do it in a single-seater . . . it just does not happen. I stayed in Bahrain that night with my team and it was great. The next thing I knew, Martin Whitmarsh from McLaren came on the phone to congratulate me and said, 'We'll discuss where we can go from here.' That was typical of Martin and Ron, they were always there somewhere in the background keeping an eye on me. They really cared and wanted to help but also wanted us to learn the hard way.

Throughout my time supported by McLaren Mercedes, a lot of people, and not only some of my competitors, disliked me for the fact that I had this McLaren contract at such a young age. Some people wanted what I had and thought it was easy for me because my racing was fully funded. But keeping a sponsor like McLaren, the biggest company in Formula One, was not exactly easy. Imagine having Ron Dennis call you, having that pressure . . . I knew if I had any problems at school or if I did not keep performing, I would lose the opportunity. Everyone said I would be nothing without McLaren – but I did not have McLaren for those two weeks in Asia. In fact, I did not have McLaren for the first five years of my racing career but I had still won championships. After a difficult weekend in

Macau, I then went out to Bahrain and proved I could win even when times were bad. I had turned things round as I had to and it was a most pleasurable feeling. I do not think for one moment that coming out of contract was just a bluff; at the time I really thought I had lost McLaren.

After Bahrain, McLaren was back on. From there, we analysed all the different options and teams in GP2 and Formula Three. I selected the teams that I was interested in and to help me form my own opinion I went to them all with a notepad and pen, as a nineteen-year-old, and asked them how they could help me win. Once we had decided what was the best option McLaren brokered an agreement with the then current Formula Three Euroseries champions ASM. ASM was and still is run and owned by Frédéric Vasseur. Frédéric is an incredible man and it was an absolutely fantastic team to work for: I learned so much from them. They were the ones who gave me the opportunity to learn how to set the car up and do what I do now in Formula One. It was great, the best year of my life outside of Formula One. I won fifteen races out of twenty. Well, I actually won sixteen, but eight of us got disqualified from the sixteenth race at Spa, something about a worn-down rear diffuser, so that took a win away.

The win I enjoyed the most was at Monaco, a track where I had always wanted to race. I got there and I was so quick. There were two races. I won the first and in the second, leading again, I hit the wall badly with five laps to go and nearly destroyed the car. When I hit the wall, the rear wheels buckled, the right pushrod was bent and the balance was all over the place. The car was really messed up. Adrian Sutil (now in Formula One with Spyker) closed the gap and he was all over me. I could not go round left-hand corners very well because my suspension was broken but through the right-handers I was okay. I had to be nervous of the kerbs, but I still won and it just felt so good.

The following year, 2006, we went to GP2, which was a completely different experience. There were quite a lot of people there who saw the McLaren name on my suit and wanted autographs and whatever. I joined the ART Grand Prix team again with Frédéric Vasseur, the owner of ASM. Nico Rosberg had won GP2 with them the year before so they were the team to be with. During the season, I remember speaking to Ron Dennis and Martin Whitmarsh and saying, 'I want to do Formula One next year, I think I'm ready.' They gave no indication this might be possible but said I had to do the job, I had to win, so you can understand the amount of pressure that I was under at the time. There was a spot that I thought had my name on it and I worked as hard as I could to get it. I kept telling Ron and Martin, 'Next year I'm going to be ready for Formula One, I promise.'

I remember that both my dad and I had no idea what was going to happen at McLaren the following year or whether I would reach Formula One or have to go elsewhere. I was performing well at that time and I was leading the GP2 Championship. My dad remained calm about my future prospects and that gave me a huge amount of confidence even though I still wanted that confirmation from McLaren. Then, the end of the season got really tough, as I battled for the title with Nelson Piquet Jr. McLaren said: 'There is a possibility that you could race with us next year.' That was it, I had to have it. The pressure was greater than ever. I eventually won GP2 and thought this is it, it's now time for McLaren to give me the opportunity, I know I can do it.

I eventually got the chance that I had been asking for to test a Formula One car. I remember I wanted to impress in my first attempt but instead I took it steady, trying not to make any mistakes but just applying myself methodically. The engineers were professionals and experienced, they could tell if I was right or not for the job – but then, after everything, I got the news that the Formula One seat was mine.

CHAPTER

DREAMS

'He [Ron Dennis] sat down and spoke to me for what seemed like ages … I got him to sign my autograph book and I said, "Can you also put down your number and address please?" and he said, "Okay … I tell you what … phone me in nine years and I will sort you out a deal".'

FOR ME IT WAS JUST A COOL NIGHT OUT.

A lot of people have talked about it since as if it was the night that changed my life. But when I left home with my dad on that first Sunday evening of December 1995, little did I know what lay ahead. I was ten years old and on my way to my first prestigious motor sport awards event – the annual Autosport Awards dinner. This was a major event that is a kind of celebration of the motor racing year gone by. It was a real big deal.

I was going because I had won the British Formula Cadet Karting Championship, my first national title. I felt proud, of course, but a bit apprehensive, too. The dinner was held at the Grosvenor House Hotel in Park Lane, London. There were about a thousand people in a huge room full of tables and chairs and there were waiters everywhere. It was amazing. I was wearing a green velvet jacket that my dad had borrowed from Mike Spencer, the previous year's winner of the British Formula Cadet Championship. Fortunately for me, he was my size, although Linda had to take up the sleeves. I borrowed his shiny patent leather black shoes off him as well. That night, just ten years old and in that suit, I felt really good, like the whole thing fitted me.

I had started to watch Formula One a few years before that evening, of course, and McLaren were the team I followed. I was just attracted by the colours of the McLaren car around that time. It was my favourite. I was a huge fan of their driver Ayrton Senna. It was a strange feeling. It was that team that made me think, 'I want to drive that car one day.' I wanted to be in that team. 'One day, I want to be in his seat.' I had always followed Senna. When I went to the Autosport Awards it was the year after he had been killed at Imola. To this day I always feel a bit gutted that I missed him by a year. He was 'the man' for me. It was everything about him, but especially the way he drove and him as a person.

Anyway, for that Autosport Awards night, my dad made me a very special autograph booklet, with spaces for people to write their names, addresses and phone numbers. It was all done out really professionally. Dad thought we might never get the chance again and so let's capture as much information and details as we can just in case we ever get the opportunity to do something with it. I still have that book at home. I carried the thing with me all night and, after the dinner, when everyone was walking around, my dad was saying, 'Oh, that's so and so, go and get their autograph.' There were all these different people and I hadn't a clue who they were. I don't think kids at that age remember names and faces particularly, but what they can remember is the number on the car, or the colour of the car, be it a rally car or whatever, and the driver's trademark helmet.

So when my dad said, 'That's Colin McRae who drives a Subaru,' I was like, 'No, really!' Colin McRae was the man at that time and he was also one of the guys I met early on who was genuine, who gave me time. That night, he gave me so much time and he was so pleasant. At the end of the awards presentation Colin, his brother Alistair and a few friends were chanting 'Lewis, Lewis!' It was incredibly funny to have these big guys shouting out my name. I really appreciated Colin from that day. Sadly, he was killed in a helicopter crash during the weekend of the Belgian Grand Prix this year. I had not seen him for a long time, but remember that he was such a great guy.

Eventually that night, my dad said, 'There's Ron Dennis, go and get his autograph.' I walked up to Ron. I remember standing in front of him. I remember being so nervous but confident at the same time; nervous of speaking, but I also had my own self-belief, too. I knew what I wanted but I was not confident that I could speak the words properly. I was uncomfortable to the point that I really did not want to say too much. So I went up to him and I said, 'Hello, I'm Lewis

Hamilton. One day I'd like to be a racing driver and I'd like to race for McLaren . . .'

Ron sat down and spoke to me for what seemed like ages, ten minutes or so, although I'm sure it was really just a minute or two. I remember looking in his eyes – and I never lost contact with him. He said, 'You have got to work hard at school. You have got to keep that spirit and keep going.' So I got him to sign my autograph book and I said, 'Can you also put down your number and address please?' and he said 'Okay.' He wrote down his address and said, 'I tell you what – phone me in nine years and I will sort you out a deal.' I said, 'Okay' and he wrote down his phone number. He just wrote, 'Call me in nine years.'

Like I said, I have still got the autograph at home and it is odd to recall, like when I looked back recently, that I got Sir John Surtees as my first autograph when my dad told me how much he had won and who he was and about his achievements; then Sir Stirling Moss, Sir Jackie Stewart and all these great people. It was so cool. I guess at ten years old I had no clue what it all really meant. I was in a complete daze.

I won several British Kart Championships in different classes after that, and so I went again to the Autosport Awards the year after and the year after that – three times in a row – and it is really a pleasure when I go now because you sit there amongst all these youngsters and you say, 'Shoot, that was me many years ago!' It is weird because when you are that age people say, 'I remember when I was your age . . .' and all that.

And now I am sitting here, and I am only twenty-two, but I am looking at the kids and I am thinking 'Wow, ten years ago . . .'

A few weeks after my third visit to the Autosport Awards, Ron Dennis's secretary, Justine, called my dad on his mobile phone. 'Hello, Anthony, Ron would like to talk to you.' My dad couldn't believe he had called. He came to me and said, 'Ron Dennis has called – and he's offered to support your career financially, technically and whatever is necessary.' I was like, 'Oh, yeah. Great.' And I just went upstairs to my room and got on with my homework – I think I was in shock! It was so unbelievable. I struggled to take it in – until my dad said he was actually going to meet with Ron later in the week.

Ron used to come to some of the kart races because he was the sponsor of the McLaren Mercedes Champions of the Future Series. I remember him coming to speak to me after I won the Cadet Championship. He smiled at me and he just said, 'It's nice to see you up here.' That was, I think, in 1996.

When I won Junior Yamaha the next year, he was there again and smiled at me on the top step of the podium and joked, 'Oh, no. Not you again!' My dad was happy when he phoned a year after that. He was ecstatic, but, for me, I was just the same. I guess that phone call changed our lives far more than I ever understood at the time, but my dad knew exactly what and how much it meant.

I was very appreciative of the opportunity, but I was not really old enough to understand it. My dad looked after all the stuff outside my racing, just as he does now in Formula One.

Though I was pleased when the McLaren drivers David Coulthard or Mika Hakkinen came to a few of the kart races, and I was obviously really impressed with their talent and achievements, I have never really been into hero worship like some people. There are those who are amazed by everything they see around these famous people and then they want to be just like these 'stars' who have become their role models. I have never been like that but maybe I would have been if I had met Ayrton Senna or if I were to meet Michael Jackson, say, I would be star-struck, but I honestly haven't been star-struck yet. I do not have a role model as such: I prefer to take a little bit from everyone, whether it is fashion, style, music or whatever.

One person who does stand out for me though is Muhammad Ali. I have never met him but would love to. When I see him on TV, I think 'Whoah, this dude . . .' He is my favourite sportsman ever. I go onto the internet and watch clips of him and I have also got the *When We Were Kings* DVD. Seeing him in the 'Rumble in the Jungle' . . . oof . . . that was sick! I love watching those kind of old-school things when you try to understand what was going on back then. How cool was Ali! I would love to be like that. No one had the balls he had. That's inspirational.

The style that Ali had and the way he was such a hero matters to me so much more than money ever could. One of the many people I have met this year, a kid no older than thirteen, asked me about being at McLaren and what it is like. He asked, 'How's the money?' Well, I can tell you I have not spent any money, or hardly any at all, and I have not even seen any money! My dad is taking care of that stuff. I spend money like I have done for the last few years – in limited amounts and for necessities only, although maybe one day I'll splash out on something for my family and myself. Ron Dennis always mentions it to me – he kids me about it. 'Oh, I know you're always pinching pennies' and I'm like, 'Hold on a sec . . . we've not had a lot of money to grow up with and I don't need to go and spend any money.' And that is right. I have a car provided for me, by Mercedes-Benz, which I am very fortunate to have. There isn't anything else that I need at the moment but if there is, it's taken care of by my dad. Honestly, there is nothing else I could possibly want. Dad and I once talked figures of what I could earn in the next few years as an Formula One driver and we could not even imagine a tiny fraction of what people say I could earn. It is just crazy.

What difference does it really make? Okay, maybe you can buy more things but what difference does that really make in your life? I don't know. I must admit, I like boats, big ones. My friend has a boat and that is just the most unreal thing. It is pretty seriously cool. So, if I were ever to save up for anything, it would be a boat. I was very fortunate to be invited to spend some of my summer holiday on a boat owned by Mansour Ojjeh and his family – it was so cool. Mansour is a shareholder in the McLaren Group.

You wake up one morning on the boat, and you can just go somewhere else. That's what we did and I loved it. Mansour has such a great family. That's why he is so happy. So, for me, it was a real pleasure to see that.

None of that would have happened, of course, if I had not been driving for McLaren and if I had not been in Formula One. So I do appreciate how lucky I am. In 1998, when I was only thirteen, I met Prince Charles when he came to visit the McLaren headquarters. And since then, I have met lots of people from all walks of life and all parts of the world. It is one of the great thrills of my job and I am truly grateful that I have had this opportunity. I am determined to make the most of it and I believe, just like I did in 1995, that if I aim for my dream then it can happen.

CHAPTER  7

RUNNING

'I was determined to succeed. I was ready to do anything it took. I knew I was young and I was a rookie. But I am very straightforward and I say what's on my mind. I will not try to be someone I am not. I will just tell it as I see it or understand it.'

AFTER MY FIRST FEW TESTS in the McLaren Formula One car, I was comfortably putting in respectable lap times during testing. I think it impressed a few people that I was consistently getting on with my job. I knew then that anything is possible. I was saying, 'You know, we can actually win a race if we work hard enough.' And that is when my road to Formula One really began. That is when a real new chapter in my life started.

I had been on that road for some time. I was running. I wanted to go to Formula One. I was pushing as hard as I could. Every opportunity I had, I told them I was ready. Then Martin Whitmarsh hinted, while I was going for the GP2 Championship title in 2006, that there was a possibility I could race in Formula One. 'But,' he said, 'if you don't win, you know, it will make it more difficult to put you in the car.' The pressure was now greater than ever. I'm sure it wasn't intentional to add more pressure but that's the way it was. I wanted it so much.

I had a period during the year when I was a bit negative and I came back positive. I had five wins, six fastest laps and took pole and the race win at Monaco in GP2. I also had a double win at Silverstone.

Eventually, at the end of September, I was called to Ron's home. Martin Whitmarsh was there. I went along with my dad and we were told that I would be racing in 2007 for Vodafone McLaren Mercedes. Well, we were kind of numb with shock. We wanted to burst out laughing, crying or whatever but we just sat there as if this sort of thing happened every day. Even when we had left and got in the car we still couldn't believe it, and it was only when we gradually got closer to home that the reality of it kicked in. The family were ecstatic! We were sworn to secrecy so couldn't share our news with anyone except Linda, Nic, my mum and her husband Ray. It was torture for a few weeks but worth it!

It was a very good year for me and, at last, I had the opportunity to test a Formula One car. It was a great feeling. Having your first test in a Formula One car, you feel that you want to blow the world away and I was really determined. But it didn't happen just like that. It took time. The team understood how tough it would be for me to begin with, so they gave me plenty of time, six or eight test days at Silverstone and then I started to find a real consistency.

My first-ever test took place at Silverstone. It was a cold grey day but the world was alight as far as I was concerned. I took it easy, not wanting to make a mistake on my first day in the job by crashing the car. My dad was petrified that I might push too hard but gradually the more laps I did the more comfortable and confident I became.

I remember that when I was first given the job, my race engineer and now good friend Phil Prew was a bit disappointed that he did not get to work on Fernando's car. He was, after all, the double World Champion. I remember he told me and I said, 'I'm sorry that you didn't get Fernando, but I'll do the best job I can.' And all credit to Phil, he was great about it after that and relished the challenge of working with a rookie. He turned out to be so very, very positive and he said, 'Don't worry. We'll work hard and we'll do fine.'

I've heard people say that in the past some drivers used to just walk into the paddock garage and get into the car and race, then afterwards get out and go home without even a word. I wanted to make sure I was not like that. I made it clear I was willing to work twice the hours, never mind the same hours, as anyone who was working in the team. I was asking: are you willing to work the amount of hours I'm willing to work?

I was determined to succeed. I was ready to do anything it took. I knew I was young and I was a rookie. But I am very straightforward and I say what's on my mind. I will not try to be someone I am not. I will just tell it as I see it or understand it. I am easy to talk to and that is important, too. I believe you have to communicate with your own team and the people around you in as normal a manner as possible. The McLaren and Mercedes-Benz engineers and staff are some of the most intelligent, hard working and loyal people I have ever met. We all have different jobs but our goal is the same – we are a team and their support has been incredible.

There are guys like my race engineer who want to work that extra bit more in order to win. But they, like any other people, need to be motivated. They need another party to work with them.

I think that you have to be completely dedicated and focused to do this job and that's where Michael Schumacher was different. I had read about Michael and I had seen how dedicated and committed he was. So, for the six months leading up to my first Grand Prix in Australia, I was in the factory every day, from eight in the morning until six or later in the evening. Ron and Martin had basically given a number of people at McLaren the task of transforming me from a GP2 driver into a Formula One driver. The aim was to make sure that I was ready to score a podium in Melbourne, even though that seemed ambitious at the time. I put in maximum effort to achieve the best I could. I worked hard with the team and they paid me back by putting in enormous efforts in return. I did two long stints of physical training and, in between, hours of working with the engineers on the car. When I went home at night, I was finished. I went to bed at eight o'clock. And it was like that for the whole six months. When the team saw that, and how enthusiastic I was, even on bad days, they could see I was totally committed.

Working as a team is critical. Okay, it's not always possible as sometimes you have to make your own decisions for the best but generally all decisions are better when they are team driven. If I had a problem with the car, I would always come back and discuss it with my team. I never blame the car or my team and it is the same with the team to me. We are all human, and we all make mistakes. If I make mistakes, I apologize. I am still learning. It is about appreciation. Firstly, I always make sure that I go into the garage, and if it's in the morning then I always say 'good morning' to them all. Secondly, I speak to everyone – not just to my engineers but to Fernando's engineers and mechanics as well.

I give them time, which is important, and I get on with them well. They do a fantastic job. I feel that for them to put 110 per cent into us as drivers, they all need to feel that we are giving 110 per cent. I know I am because I am committed to the success and achievements of the team. For me, working as a part of the team rather than an individual in the team is the way it should be and everyone benefits from the relationship and shares in the good and the bad times as a team.

I do my best to learn from mine and other people's mistakes, whether I am right or wrong, and I try to take all that in and to mould myself so I am a better person and a more rounded driver. I feel that we are all in it together, we are a team, and without their commitment at every pit stop, I will not get out that fraction of a second quicker to get in front of someone else. Also, I feel very much involved with them as people. We are all in it together. I think, 'Come on guys, let's do this!' Sometimes, it feels a bit awkward because there are so many of them to talk to, but it helps me. It helps me feel real and keeps me in touch so that we can work together.

Earlier in the year there was a story going around saying my success was the work of other people who trained my mind, put me on the simulator and taught me how to race. I have got to say that is complete bull! And it was a rubbish story. Sure, I worked on the simulator and used it, but I knew how to race, I'd been doing it successfully for fourteen years previously. I knew how to prepare mentally and physically, and how to race, how to win and just as important how to lose a long time before I went near the simulator. Through-out my career I developed these skills with my dad's help. It is my dad's mental strength and thought process that has helped me develop myself and my application to racing and life.

In the winter after GP2, and before Formula One, I worked like I had never worked before. The team and I did everything possible for me to prepare myself in every way for the season ahead – training hard, physically and mentally. I was really feeling confident about my fitness and working on learning everything I could about the car. So, all that stuff about me being a 'robot' or simulator-trained driver is total and utter fanciful reporting.

Like all Vodafone McLaren Mercedes drivers, I have been helping to develop the simulator at McLaren on and off in recent years. It is an advanced bit of equipment, but they have been developing it since I was fifteen and it is an ongoing thing. Occasionally, I would have the opportunity to get into the simulator and just have fun, and had to take days off college to do it. It was an opportunity for me to learn more about the controls on the car and spend more time at the factory. It was also hopefully a chance to impress the bosses at McLaren and show them I could handle everything they wanted to throw my way. I wanted to be noticed so that I could get the opportunity I so desperately wanted – to drive the Formula One car.

For the past two years, I've had a great team helping me to develop and be prepared for a career in Formula One – my family, Ron Dennis, Martin Whitmarsh (McLaren's Chief Operating Officer), Norbert Haug (Vice President of Mercedes-Benz), Dr Aki Hinsta (the team's head of Human Performance), my physiotherapist and personal trainer Adam Costanzo, plus all the staff at McLaren and Mercedes-Benz. It was a full team effort.

During my training and development, I visited all the different departments and engineers both at McLaren in Woking and Mercedes-Benz in Brixworth, England and Stuttgart, Germany so I could learn about the brakes, suspension, rear-suspension geometry, disc-control settings, gear ratios, pit stop strategies, the controls, the dashboard, the launch procedure, the default procedures when you are out on the track . . . I had to take in all these different things. I had to understand them and the details and exactly how it all works and know them backwards. I took that opportunity with both hands and max-imized my potential. I did not just turn up in a daze. I went home and I studied. All the sheets of paper and booklets that they gave me, I read and made sure I understood. I had never done anything like that in my life before, but I did it then. So, it is not about being programmed. I was given an opportunity to learn and I took it. I applied myself better than I have ever applied myself – and that is why when I got to my first Grand Prix I was ready.

The only other influence on how I learned to win and learned to drive was through my experiences in karting – and through what I took from my family. I am the way I am because of my family. That is the fire in my heart. We – my family and I – have taken the opportunity presented to us and made it happen.

That fire in me is important because it drives me on. Wherever I am, if I have an idea of something that would help the team, I call them to discuss my thoughts or we talk about how it has been going so far. I might say, 'This has made a big impact here, this has helped there, this is what we need to do, this is where we are going . . .'

There are so many people who work in the factory. I try to get around as many different departments as I can – not all in one day, obviously, because there are too many, but bit by bit

I try to get to each shop, like the machine shop, and spend five or ten minutes there. It is good for me. We talk and they come over and ask me a load of questions. They are happy to hear what has been going on. I can speak to them freely because I have known them for years. I think they appreciate it as well.

I knew it was really important to prepare for everything last winter before the season began. And, for me, that meant listening to advice on food, fitness and rest and learning from it. I worked with Dr Aki and Adam and they were fantastic for me, really committed, so enthusiastic. They helped me a lot and we are like a team together. I could feel that they wanted me to win as much as I did myself. And that kind of support is a really great feeling. It is how I feel about the guys in the factory and the guys in the race team.

Dr Aki and Adam told me about this energy thing – that we all have a certain amount of energy and that some days we feel tired and some days we do not. Well, I do not claim to understand it all, but I know that food makes a big difference to the way you feel. And relaxing properly, not wasting energy when you have some to spare, is important, too.

I took that stuff on board so I was trying not to waste my energy for weeks, or months, in preparation for the new season. I knew it was going to be a really intense year. Everyone has the same schedule, but for me is was important to perform with 100 per cent mental capacity as the physical demands of racing for an hour and a half, seventeen or eighteen times a year, require your undivided attention. It is something very special. I knew that and I wanted to be ready for it.

Most people can just go through their lives and balance everything and it's really good for them and they get time to recuperate at weekends. But I am racing on average every two weeks and have been for the past fourteen years. So, in that time when I was getting ready for the season, I was coming back home and getting to bed early and getting up at a decent time and eating healthily and really taking care of myself. I am not one of those people that says that you have to eat this or that type of food all the time. Obviously, I do watch my diet, but I love the occasional bacon sandwich and a chance to enjoy some food just for the taste when I can.

I like to have a healthy balance between work and play. I have to feel free and able to do the things that I want to do. If I want to drive to London or see my friends, I know I can. If I want to go to the cinema or go bowling, I can do those sorts of things. But I also know, when I am in a racing car, it is important to be fitter than my competitors. And that comes from the preparations long in advance of the season starting. When you are racing, and you have been driving for, say, forty minutes, you start to fatigue and then your body starts to take energy from your mind. Your concentration drops and you cannot push as much and your performance just gets worse. I always train to make sure I've got enough to go for ninety minutes or more, so when I do a race I never get to the point where I know my body is fatiguing and taking energy from my mind.

You cannot brake as late or overtake as much if your brain energy is sapped away.

My life has changed so much in the last two years that it is hard to even imagine now what it used to be like. My dad manages everything and this takes all the worry away from me so that I can focus on what I do best. All my days are planned out in advance. I have a carefully fixed schedule. I have no issues to deal with. I can just have fun which means getting in that McLaren car and racing it. When I have to do appearances, I can tell people my story and enjoy it. I try to feel happy because that is what I can take energy from.

It is a great package right now for my life. Linda looks after all my diary and makes sure everything is booked – and all I have to do is arrive and drive. Of course, it wasn't always like that! But now I need to be in the best condition I can for every race. I have to be at my peak and all the stuff I have learned in the past has to come out now. I try to avoid making any mistakes and I feel able to do that because everything around me is right. So much of it is in the preparation. That's why I went back to those basic principles when I was working all last winter down in Woking, reading, absorbing and learning – and training so hard I was ready for anything that lay ahead when I caught the plane to Melbourne.

CHAPTER **8**

UNBELIEVABLE!

'I was standing on the podium thinking … "I've done my parents proud." I had been so busy all weekend that I had hardly spoken to my dad … we never seemed to have more than five minutes together. Seeing his expression after the race made it worth all the effort. "My dad's smiling down there," I thought, "so I know he's happy – and that's all that matters to me. There's one thing I can do that makes my dad smile and this is it."'

I DO NOT KNOW HOW MANY LAPS I LED FOR, but it was a few . . . And, right there and then, on those laps, I knew I was just meant to be in Formula One. I could feel it.

For years, I had played all these Grand Prix games. I had been everywhere on all the circuits, racing against Nic on the computer. And here I was in Australia, in Melbourne, and this time it was for real. It had felt great enough to be running second, in my debut race, so when McLaren told me over the radio, 'Lewis, you're now leading,' I was like 'Shoooooooot – I'm leading my first Grand Prix. How wicked is that!' I just loved that moment. I wish I could live it forever, again and again. The reaction afterwards was something else, too, but it was that race, and the whole weekend, that brought it all home for me. My first event, the Australian Grand Prix: to finish on the podium there was just fantastic.

Right from the start, I knew I was fit and I was ready. I flew out to Australia with Adam. I had already started working with him in 2006 when he helped me prepare for the final few races of the GP2 season, making sure that I maintained my fitness. When Martin Whitmarsh asked me what I thought of having Adam as my personal trainer, I said, 'We get on really well. He's very enthusiastic. It would be cool.' So, together, we did all the pre-season training and, knowing the level of dedication that he had put in over that period of time, I was confident before that first race. Adam was so passionate about his job. He would say, 'We want to win!' and for someone whom I had known for only a short period of time, this was amazing. I felt so lucky to have found someone like that, where you just click and get on with it.

I was glad to feel so well prepared. It helped there and then as much as anywhere else. The whole Formula One experience is so intense, especially at the first race of the season. It is a lot more intense in terms of physical training and preparing mentally and also in terms of other things like the winter testing programme, which was pretty hectic. I needed to squeeze as many running miles in through the winter as possible. For me, that meant running three days a week after coming in from GP2. At the same time, I did a lot of physical exercise work with Adam to make sure I felt fresh and confident. Then, before the race, I started going to sleep at a different time every night, bit by bit during the week, to prepare for the time difference. Adam then flew to Australia and a few days later I followed him.

I stopped off in Hong Kong, partly to break up the journey and partly to see Jodia Ma, my ex-girlfriend. I spent a couple of days with her at her house; we went into town, around Hong Kong, took the trip to Macau, and went around the circuit I had raced on in Formula Three, one of my favourite circuits in the world. It was just that: a nice break on the journey with a very good friend. I had broken up with Jo in January, just before my birthday, when it was obvious that my schedule was not going to give me time to include her. I had told her that I faced a very intense time, that I had to go away the week of my birthday for a week of special training in Finland, and was due to come back for one day and then go to Spain, for three days of testing. Then when I came back again, I had two more days of special training and then I was due to fly out some-where else the next day.

I explained it was going to be like that all the way to the first race. I knew also that her parents needed her back home – so I said, 'You know, Jo, it is best to be around the family when needed . . . Maybe you should go back to Hong Kong.' I knew it would be hard for her. I said, 'I'm going to be away for the first Grand Prix, then I'm going to be away two months and you're just going to be here in London.' In the end, we sorted it out and we went our separate ways. She left London and went back to start her life again in Hong Kong. It was hard not having Jo around but we kept in contact.

I first met Jo at a party in London. She had actually been at Cambridge Arts and Sciences College in 2003, a year behind me, where she'd become good friends with one of my best mates, Mohammed. There was just something about her that I really liked and I found myself meeting up with her all the time. She was such a kind, considerate person that she became a really big part of my life. I had never before had the opportunity or desire outside of my racing to spend time with such a loving and generous girl like Jo. She had to cope with a lot, living and studying in England and being away from her family, which was difficult for her. In 2004 her family's business sponsored my racing in Macau. Unfortunately, the business suffered a downturn in fortune in 2005 and the family could no longer support her studying in England and she had to return home.

In November 2005, after a race in Macau, Jo flew back with me to London but she was stopped at customs and not allowed back in the country because she had only two weeks remaining on her visa. She said she was about to renew it for her studies, but instead of letting her in, the customs officers boxed her in a room and then sent her back on a flight that night. It took her two months to sort that out, but she came back on my birthday after renewing her visa. It was a nice present, but it was only temporary as her family still needed her support and so she returned to Hong Kong shortly after.

After a while, Jo moved with her mother and sister to Atlanta, in Georgia, to stay with friends while the family business was wound down. Around that time, I took a flight over to the US in the middle part of my GP2 season, stayed with her in Atlanta and then took a road trip with her and her sister, seven hours, down to New Orleans and to Florida. It was really cool – Orlando, Disneyworld and all that stuff.

Apart from her studies, I was the only other reason Jo returned to the UK after that and it was a big weight on my shoulders. If a girl does something like that, then it is a real commitment. It became serious and very intense. I was beginning to worry about how I could share my time between the two things I loved. I had always told Jo that I could never let anything affect my racing and it was coming to the point where our relationship just could not continue for that reason. She knew it. It was an incredibly tough time but we both had to be mature and face the realities of our lives, where we lived and what we wanted to achieve. Maybe it was just the wrong time to meet such a fantastic lady and her family. We still have a great friendship.

After the stopover in Hong Kong I flew down to Brisbane, where Adam comes from and where his family live. Brisbane was quite unreal. I had never been to Australia before and when I got there, it seemed so familiar and similar to everything I had seen and read. I felt great, in a great place and probably because I was with Adam I felt like I was at home. After a day or two, we flew up to the Gold Coast and stayed in a hotel where we concentrated on our training programme. It was about sleeping right and making sure my body was prepared and had recovered from the jet lag. Everything was perfect.

When we flew down to Melbourne, it was so nice. It was my first Grand Prix, of course, and there were a lot of events for me to do with the sponsors, the team and the media. It was my first experience of what to expect at a Grand Prix. We went to the track and I did some preparation with my team, walked the circuit and just soaked it up. I was picked up in a car and taken to the hotel where I had my own S-class Mercedes, which was cool. I was staying in this great hotel and could feel some of the expectation building. I just tried to stay calm and focused.

I learned so much that weekend – not just on the track, but off it as well. The schedule, the intensity, the pressure – I had to take it all in and handle it. I was being whisked everywhere: up in the morning, go to the track, do this and do that, then I was pulled away to a promotional event – it was just relentless but really enjoyable for me, too. On the Friday, I had the driver's briefing with my engineer, then I was able to get onto the track, then it was lunchtime, then I was out testing again. When I finished, I had an engineers' meeting for an hour or two, then a briefing for all the drivers after which I had to rush back to the hotel, change quickly into my suit and go to this event, at the top of a tall building, where I had to stand on a box in front of a big crowd and talk with a microphone . . . For me, it was my first event like that in front of so many people. I had done the Vodafone McLaren Mercedes launch in Valencia, obviously, and that was almost unreal, too, so here I was just standing there talking. They were a great audience, and I had a good time.

There was also so much to learn technically about a Formula One car that I was pleased I had done all those hours and hours of studying in advance. My GP2 car had nothing like the technical complexities of my Formula One car. In GP2, you do not have traction control or numerous knobs and buttons on the steering wheel like in Formula One, so for me it was something new to try to get used to traction control and being able to use the differential for braking by adjusting a switch on the steering wheel. I have twenty buttons on the steering wheel, and for me that was the hardest part of my learning curve going into Formula One – understanding what effect and function each setting had on the performance of the car and how to optimize them. But after that first day in Melbourne, I felt that it was pretty similar in a lot of ways to all the other tests I had done.

So I did all the preparations and I went out on the Friday – and I did not put it in the wall! I thought I did a reasonable job and kept out of trouble. There had been a lot of talk down the years and finally, when I got this job, people were saying things like, 'Oh well, he's not going to be able to do it.' I think even Ron Dennis was conservative about it. 'You'll be alright,' he said. 'You'll finish in the top ten.' Did Ron underestimate me? I don't know, I think he was just trying to manage my expectations in preparation for any possible disappointment.

Most other people did, though, understandably given that I was a rookie about to race a Vodafone McLaren Mercedes Formula One car.

That first day round Albert Park in free practice I finished up P3. It was just a fantastic day for me. To leave the garage for the first time in Melbourne and drive down the pit straight was, for me, living my dream. I had been getting up early for years to watch this race and now I was in it. It rained at the start and that made the circuit a bit slippery and more difficult to learn. Any wet circuit is a bit tricky, but Melbourne was a street circuit with a lot of white lines around. I had to watch out for them. It went pretty smoothly, especially in the second session when we made some progress, and I finished that first day feeling pretty strong. Fernando had finished seventh.

After the sessions, I was asked to attend my first official Formula One news conference upstairs in the media centre. That was pretty cool, too. There were five of us, I think: myself, Heikki Kovalainen, Jenson Button, Mark Webber and David Coulthard. Me and Heikki sat in the front row and I think we got most of the questions! I remember one of them was about the jump up from GP2 to Formula One.

The next day, Saturday, I went into my first Formula One qualifying session and ended up fourth on the grid. That meant I was in the second row for my first Grand Prix start: P4. I said I was overwhelmed and it was true. I was enjoying every moment of the whole experience, but a little part of me was disappointed that I had not outqualified my team-mate

Fernando, even if he was the World Champion. I always want to come out on top if I can and I think it is natural for any racing driver.

On race day, Sunday, obviously I was a bit nervous before the start, but nothing more than was usual, I felt. When the lights went out, I got off pretty well. I was on the dirty side of the grid, but I had as good a start, reaction-wise, as Fernando, but he had better traction. That meant he could pull away and I came under attack from the cars around and behind me as I went into the first corner.

Robert Kubica, in his BMW, came round the outside and slotted in front of me and took my place. I had a moment when I reacted and I thought, 'Shoot, if I stay in this spot, there's gonna be a few other cars that will go round the outside . . . I'll be down in eighth . . . I'm gonna come out a lot further back than where I started and that's not good – and I'm not having it!' There was no reason for me to stay in that queue. So, before everyone started braking, it was *Boom! Dice to the outside, to the left.* Then, they started braking and I'm still on the power. *Dice more, down to the left.* I braked. I do not even know how I judged where I was, braking-wise. And then, there was a gap around the outside of Fernando! I just slotted in so perfectly.

I did lose a bit of 'aero' from my front wing because I touched Nick Heidfeld's BMW, his wheel clipping my front wing and breaking something. Otherwise, I could have been even quicker. But it was all happening, all at once. Then, I looked in my mirrors and I could see everything. 'Shoot! I just overtook that whole pack and I've got Fernando behind me . . .' It was a heart-pounding moment for me. I was really in it. I was in the middle of everything. I had just overtaken Fernando, the World Champion, with an outside manoeuvre and it was one of those feelings where you are really right on the limit. You either pull it off or you don't. And, realistically, there was far more chance of me not pulling that off, but it all went so well. And it was not luck. I just timed it to perfection and I got in there and I was like, 'Phew! That's a much better place to start!'

I was third, working on overtaking Nick Heidfeld in front – and he was lighter on fuel than me so there was no way I was going to catch him. But I knew he was going to stop early so that was cool. The key for me was just keeping Fernando in my mirror – and in the distance. So I pulled out a gap and then I would get round a corner, pull a few hundred metres and look in my mirror and if Fernando was in the same place, or further behind, I knew it was alright. That's how I judge the distance. Then it was just, 'Keep pushing and don't make mistakes . . .' That's what I concentrated on doing. I did my best, but I got caught up in traffic before I pitted and finished third.

I was gutted that I didn't beat Fernando but I thought 'he is a great driver and a double World Champion' and I have to give him credit for his drive. I felt so much satisfaction at finishing third in my first Grand Prix. When I stepped onto the podium, it felt almost like winning a race. It was very emotional because of what I had gone through in the previous six months, what my family had done, how much work we had all put in. It had all come together and I felt really full with it all.

Then, other thoughts started entering my mind, like 'Is this a one-off thing? How do I maintain it?' I was standing on the podium thinking that, but at the same time feeling great and thinking 'I've done my parents proud.' I had been so busy all weekend that I had hardly spoken to my dad. He was there in Melbourne, staying in another hotel nearby, but we never seemed to have more than five minutes together. Seeing his expression after the race made it worth all the effort. 'My dad's smiling down there,' I thought, 'so I know he's happy – and that's all that matters to me. There's one thing I can do that makes my dad smile and this is it.'

I knew that after that, things would change. I knew then that everyone would know who I was. It made things harder. I had earned respect, but I was not going out there to earn respect. I was out there to win. There is no doubt that the result was very much a turning point for me, even more so when I think about it now. It was a reward for both me and my dad and a great start to the year. It was a foundation stone for what lay ahead. My hard work and all my preparations with Adam had paid off. I knew we had done as much running as we could in pre-season testing and I had done plenty of race distances, so I knew I was fit enough. It was just another learning curve for me.

You get confidence every time you finish a race. You gain a bit of confidence in the car. You know what you can do with it. I knew what I needed to do. It was good to have that first race under my belt, over and done with. And now, after so many months of hard work, I had a chance to go and let my hair down and have a bit of fun for a few days before the next race.

Actually, I had a three-week break before the next event, in Malaysia, but in the middle of the second week there was a three-day test at the Sepang Circuit, near Kuala Lumpur International Airport. There was no point flying all the way back home and then back to Malaysia. I decided it was a chance to go to some places I'd always wanted to see. I went to Bangkok for two days with Adrian Sutil, who is a great friend of mine, and from there we went to Koh Samui. It was my first break after all the build-up to Australia. It was great fun. I enjoyed the sights and the food was really good, too. After Koh Samui, we did the three-day test and from there, with Adam and Adrian, I also met up with Jo in Bali. We all had a great time.

Then we returned to Malaysia for the race and Jo went home to Hong Kong. Kuala Lumpur is a really cool city. It is modern with a lot of interesting old districts, and the atmosphere, the food and the weather are all just great. I was feeling good, very confident and enjoying the whole vibe. The circuit, at Sepang, near the airport, is a big and modern place with a wide track, good for the cars. It has plenty of room, but the heat is just amazing. Someone once said that racing in Sepang is like racing in a sauna and that is just exactly right. It really is so hot.

I had done well in Melbourne and I wanted to prove myself again. I had a feeling that I could do more and do better, but I was not given the best chance in qualifying. In the end, Fernando was second on the grid, sharing the front row with Felipe Massa's Ferrari, after Felipe took pole, and I was fourth, next to Kimi Räikkönen in the other Ferrari. It was obviously going to be a pretty tense start with both Ferraris and McLarens all together like that at the front. And it was.

I had a pretty good getaway and so did Fernando. He was able to pass Felipe and I managed to pass both Ferraris before the first corner. I think Felipe was paying a bit too much attention to Kimi and that gave us a chance. I did not need asking twice and I went straight through with Fernando. It was a bit like Melbourne, another chance to take some places and I did it. It meant that I had to cope with some pressure, too. It was something else, something new for me. It was the most difficult race I had ever been in: I had both of those Ferraris behind me, two big red blobs in my mirrors, and I had to try to make sure they stayed there. It was so difficult. I knew they were lighter than me and that they were faster than me.

Felipe made a couple of moves to pass me, into turn four, I think. I was lucky because I was able to lead him into a mistake – and it was lucky, too, that I was able to cut back across in front of him and in the end, eventually, he went off. It was really dicey stuff and I remember I apologized for it after the race at the press conference and everybody laughed. At the end of the day, we got the points because I came home second behind Fernando, who had been able to pull clear and build a lead, but the thing I always remember from that race was the heat and the pressure. I had Kimi right behind me, too, hunting me down, and it was just so tough. Inside that cockpit, I was sweating so much and halfway through the race I ran out of water.

It was tricky. I kept pushing all the time, just to hold them off and to stay in front of them all the way to the last lap. It would have been nice if I had been further ahead in the final stint, but I had to put up with it. I concentrated on not making any mistakes and the team did the rest. The car was really good. The team did a fantastic job and they deserved the rewards because they work such long hours. I felt proud to be on the podium again, really thrilled to be second. But a part of me always wants to win and as always I wanted to beat my teammate, so in that way, while I was happy, I was just a bit disappointed to be behind Fernando but I remained confident that it would just be a matter of time until I gained the necessary experience to be in front.

I knew it was not going to be easy, in my first season, and that you cannot predict what is going to happen. Testing is one thing and racing is another. I was quick enough and I knew I was very strong at racing so that was not an issue. We did longer stints and race runs in testing, but it is a lot different to actually doing it in a race when you have someone pressuring you like that and there is no room for error. All that said, though, I was still delighted to get two podiums in my first two races.

A lot of people were interested in how I managed to shake off Felipe when he attacked me. On the exit of turn two, I knew he was close and he seemed to be extremely quick down the straight. So I expected him to be slipstreaming me going into turn four. I did move over, but not too far. I did not want to compromise my exit. Then, he dived and I anticipated that and tried to brake as late as possible. All those old lessons from my dad came into my instinctive reactions I guess. I tried to outbrake him but he braked even later than me! But I was able to get the car into the corner and he was lost – he was going straight! He was gone. And then I knew that each time, as soon as we braked, he was going to overshoot so I was able to control the car and keep ahead. It was definitely my hardest battle up to that time. I had a great sense of achievement after that, but I was itching for my first win. That Sunday night I went to a Kanye West concert with my dad and Adam to celebrate – that was awesome.

Those two early results – third in Australia and second in Malaysia – had given me a real confidence boost and there was a lot of talk about me going one step higher. Sure, I wanted to do that, but it is always dangerous to talk like that and make predictions. I was aware of that from my own mistakes and from my own career. I have always been fortunate, along the way, that whenever I have gone to a new category I have usually been able to challenge at the front. That is down to having a good team and a good, competitive car.

To be honest, I had always found that I had a decent amount of respect from the other drivers throughout my career. I felt it was the same in Formula One, but obviously I was still new and I was learning my way around. I had not spent that much time on track racing against a lot of the other drivers so it was difficult to know how far they would go in certain situations. I just had to pay them respect and hope for the same in return. I had experienced so much in just two races, especially in Malaysia, in my tussle with the Ferraris, and Felipe in particular, that I had learned a lot of that stuff. But I knew there were tough challenges ahead and I was not going to make predictions. In racing, anything can happen.

The next day, we went to Bahrain, a place I knew because I had raced there before. As I took a look at the Sakhir track for the next race, I was trying to be careful not to be drawn in. I did not want to be making mistakes in or out of the car. I was enjoying the banter with Felipe and that was cool. He seemed to be a straight guy and we got along well. I felt he was open and easy to be with, too, in spite of the way we had battled in Malaysia. He was also very fast!

Again, a lot of the media were turning the spotlight on me. There were lots of questions from the local journalists, and as always a lot from the international media who travel to

Focusing, waiting, watching …

Out in front, I enjoyed leading the field at Donington Park in this Formula Renault UK race in 2003.

Above I ran my first season of Formula Renault UK in 2002 and finished third.

Below left In 2005 I won at every circuit in the F3 Euroseries.

Below centre Racing on the streets of Macau in the Formula Three event in 2004.

Below right My F3 win in Bahrain, from the back, was an important statement of intent for me.

Above Formula Renault Eurocup success.

Above Discussing GP2 with McLaren's Martin Whitmarsh.

Above Crossing the line and winning the GP2 Championship at Monza in 2006.

Right The race to win – Monaco GP2, 2006.

Winning at home in front of the British fans is a fabulous feeling and I loved it at Silverstone, where I won the GP2 race in 2006.

Left My first Formula One seat and car fitting in the McLaren factory.

Right Fans surprise me at Melbourne Park ahead of my first Australian Grand Prix.

Below Preparing my mind – eyes closed as I focus on the job ahead before the Australian Grand Prix.

Above Arriving with Fernando for a Vodafone promotion on St Kilda beach, Melbourne, Australia.

Left Hold it high – celebrating my first podium finish in my maiden Formula One outing at the Australian Grand Prix this year.

Below Spinning a few friendly words with Australian bowling legend Shane Warne.

Above The Spanish Grand Prix, and a dramatic start as I move up from fourth to second at the first corner.

Above Malaysia and a team one-two – fantastic!

Right Three wise men – my dad Anthony with Dave Ryan, McLaren team manager, and Ron Dennis, the boss.

Above Sharing a smile with Felipe Massa in Bahrain, my third straight podium finish.

'Monaco pit stop – a team effort!'

all the races. People wanted to know how I was coping with the pressure and the level of expectation and stuff like that. I just told them it felt natural to me because, honestly, it did. I was feeling very happy to be there and said I had worked for thirteen years to get my chance. And I wanted to carry on enjoying it by performing as well as I could.

I felt good. I was in my third Grand Prix and they were all very different. I do not think you could get three more contrasting places really than Australia, Malaysia and then Bahrain – and the ways the people dressed in places as different as the Gold Coast beaches and the Arabian deserts showed that, too. But while that was interesting, and stimulating, I knew I had to concentrate on my job. And I knew that in the race, I had to be very careful in the first corner, a tight and tricky one, where anything could happen.

I really wanted to do well again, of course, but more than anything I wanted a chance to prove that I could beat Fernando on the day and in a straight fight. The practice sessions on Friday went well and then on Saturday, in qualifying, I wound up two places ahead of him. Again, Felipe took pole for Ferrari, but this time I was second and Fernando was fourth – it was a straight turnaround of positions for us from Malaysia. On Sunday I knew the start was going to be vital again and I just built up my concentration on the grid. My dad was holding a parasol overhead to keep me out of the heat, and the funny thing was, Rory Bremner, the British impressionist, took a walk around my car out on the grid! When the race started, I was away pretty well while Fernando came past Kimi to take third behind me.

There was an early collision, involving two cars, and this meant the Safety Car came out. After that, it was just me and Felipe in front, and we had a really close scrap, but I just could not find a way to get near enough to pass him. Then, after I pitted, my second set of tyres were just not performing for me and I lost touch a bit with Felipe who pulled away. My third set were a lot better and I pushed hard, but this time Felipe was in front and he stayed there, and stayed cool, to win the race. Fernando finished fifth.

As I was slowing down, the team came on the radio and said: 'Leading the championship, Lewis . . . Not bad for a rookie.' It was an amazing day for me. I was level top of the points table with Fernando and Kimi, all three of us having collected twenty-two, but all the attention was on me.

I cannot say I minded that. I had spent more than half of my life working for that moment, to be on top of the Drivers' Championship one day, and I loved it. It was sweet. I did my job and then I had another job to do – fly back across the world to Shanghai for another special promotional event. I literally flew directly there, walked off the plane and went straight through immigration and into the Hilton hotel, where they were all waiting. I had to get up and pour this bottle of Mobil 1 oil and talk about it. It was a real job for me so I had been reading all about Mobil 1 oil, about its qualities and so on, on the plane. There was no time to celebrate at all, even if

I had been inclined that way. You have always got to come across properly, get the message right and give a good impression at these events with the McLaren partners. And after I had spoken, I had to sit down and do interviews. I do not know how many I did that day, but it was so intense. I was glad when it was over and I could go home for a few days. I needed a rest. What I did not realize was that while I was away, a lot of things had changed.

CHAPTER

FORMULA FAME

'I like and admire Fernando, so I was sad and
disappointed that for whatever reason our relationship
did not improve but it was not for lack of trying.'

IN THE SPACE OF SIX WEEKS, MY LIFE HAD CHANGED.

I was a prisoner in my own home . . . and all because I was leading the Formula One Drivers' Championship.

I had finished third, second and then second again and I felt great. Life was so sweet. But when I returned to the UK and went to my parents' home, there were people everywhere: reporters outside and photographers camped on our doorstep. At one point, there were ten cars parked outside the house. And all because of me.

My dad warned me about the paparazzi using long-distance lenses and trying to take pictures of me. I had to keep a low profile. The reality of my situation had just set in. It was like I could not just be normal anymore. I had been away for about two months and had absolutely no idea of what had been going on back home. I had no idea of what to expect.

People, complete strangers, knew who I was. When I went to the petrol station, they were coming up to me and it was like, 'Hey, Lewis, well done and good luck.' What a strange feeling that everyone I met had been following my racing exploits both on the TV and in the papers. Some people would shout, 'You were in the papers today, well done' and so on, but unless you are there and you see it yourself, you do not know what the effect at home really has been.

For me, that was a lot even then, but it was nothing compared to what came later as the year unfolded. It was like a snowball going down a mountain – and the mountain was Everest! It just got bigger, and bigger, and bigger. My ordinary life ended then really.

I had not seen my family, other than my dad, for all that time and Nic was amazed at everything. I spoke to them, of course, from every race. They always said they couldn't believe how qualifying had gone and then how the race had gone. I knew that every weekend they had all the family round and would sit and watch the whole weekend.

I would speak to them each time before I went out for qualifying or for the race and I could hear them all. It was strange, too, with the time differences, but I could just feel the support and draw on it. It really made a huge difference for me.

So when I finally returned to the UK, we had a family reunion and a really great family meal together – our usual slow roast barbequed Sunday beef fillet prepared by dad,

Linda's special roast potatoes with Yorkshire pudding, and all the trimmings. That food, my family . . . all of that gives me such a great lift. That kind of feeling is great for energy and confidence, especially as I was more and more being drawn into a scrap at the front – not just with the two Ferraris, but also with my team-mate.

Fernando, I am sure, did not like me doing so well and getting all the attention so early in the season. That is only natural – I am sure I would feel the same in a similar situation. He really kept to himself and it was the same for me. Ron kept asking me if I would try extra hard to help Fernando feel welcome. I wanted Fernando to feel normal in the team and around me and couldn't understand why he didn't, as he never really spoke to me. I had already made a huge effort when Fernando joined the team and felt I was doing as much as I could but without a response. Nevertheless I continued to try.

Fernando is very, very quiet. You say, 'Hi', he says, 'Hello' – and that's it. I started going into his room to play computer games with him, just to build up the relationship. I took the initiative. I had to do it all and I think that if I had not gone in there and spoken to him, there would have been no relationship at all to work with. And, for the sake of the team, I knew we needed one. We all had to work together. I like and admire Fernando, so I was sad and disappointed that for whatever reason our relationship did not improve but it was not for lack of trying.

It was weird. I was pretty well bedded into the team and Fernando arrived as the two-time World Champion. I thought he would be the one trying to set me an example and show me what to do, not the other way around. I thought, 'I need to make an effort to go over and meet all the people at McLaren to win their trust and belief, and to share their motivation.' It doesn't matter what sport it is. When I used to play football, I really worked hard to meet up with the guys and when I was on the field I was enthusiastic – 'Well played!' and all that stuff. You have to work at it. You do not really know if you are doing well or not, but you need someone to be the strength of the team. That's what I felt in football even though I wasn't the captain. I was offered a chance to be captain, but I was really the central midfield guy and I was the magnet to bring the team forward. We did not always win, but that is how I felt in my team, how I feel in any team.

At the beginning of the year in January, there was a fitness week that the team had really worked hard to put together. It was for everyone, including all the mechanics from my car and Fernando's and the engineers as well. We went to Finland and it was a real bonding week for us all. Everyone went: me, test driver Pedro de la Rosa, the mechanics and engineers – everyone except Fernando. He was supposed to go, but he didn't. He didn't go so he didn't build any bond with the team. We went ten-pin bowling, we did all these team events – it was really good fun. We all enjoyed it. The only time you ever see that sort of team event normally is when you watch a film or a television programme. Often it is with soldiers and they have to do this and that and it can make a huge difference. It did for me. I think the respect I had for them and the respect they had for me grew and it was good for all of us.

So after the first three races, in which I had done pretty well with three podiums, I was feeling good. But I knew that the next race, the Spanish Grand Prix, was Fernando's home event so he was going to have that extra boost, a bit more confidence and support. It made no difference to me, or my preparations. I was just going to do my job: stay focused, think about my racing and do my level best.

The track, the Circuit de Catalunya, is about half-an-hour's drive out of the city of Barcelona, inland a bit, and a bit exposed. It can get pretty breezy there sometimes and it can also be hot. But it is the same for everybody and just about everyone in Formula One has been there to do loads of pre-season testing so it is not a place with many surprises. I went into the weekend knowing that Fernando was the likely favourite, the driver who was supposed to take the team to the World Championship. As it was his home country, I understood that he would have liked to be on pole and to be given the best shot to win the race.

On Friday, in practice, I was quickest in the morning, but I slipped to fifth in the afternoon after I ran off and picked up some dirt. It was no big deal. We were confident about the speed in the car and felt that we had taken a step ahead of Ferrari in the long break since Bahrain. More than anything, I felt

I was able to be consistent and that was important. I could see Fernando was relieved to be quickest in the afternoon and in a funny way I was pleased for him.

In qualifying, I was fourth, Felipe was on pole, Fernando was second and Kimi was third. I got a good start and got ahead of Kimi. At the first corner, I had another opportunity. Fernando had gone off in his battle with Felipe. I could see that he was coming back on to the circuit and it was very close. Fernando could have taken me out and I was like, 'Shoot!' But I got past him and then I was chasing Felipe.

I couldn't catch him, but importantly for me I stayed in front of Fernando. I was not thinking, 'I've beaten Fernando in his home country' or anything like that. It made no difference to me what country we were in – his, mine, or someone else's. I race to win wherever I am. I got the points and I was leading the championship. That was sweet. I was the youngest leader of the title race in the history of Formula One, breaking the record set by Bruce McLaren – the founder of the team I was racing for. He was a month older than me when he did it. I was twenty-two years, four months and six days old. Wow, it was cool.

I kept on telling everyone I was living my dream. To be a rookie who leads the championship after just four races was simply amazing. I had thirty points and that was two more than Fernando, who had won the title the two previous years. In so many ways, it was incredible. But in other ways, for me and my dad, and all my family, it was just what dad had always worked for. Obviously I felt happy, but after every race the dream got bigger and bigger. I knew that there was a long way to go and I did not want to start talking about winning the championship or anything like that. But I knew inside me that if we could keep the consistency going, maintain the fantastic reliability and stay out of trouble – well, then anything could happen.

I also knew that Felipe was going to be a tough competitor. I felt we had the pace of the Ferraris that weekend in Spain and I told him afterwards that we would be beating them soon. We had some good banter. He is a good guy and we get on well. That is why I was able to joke with him in Malaysia. We had started building up a friendship the year before, when I was in GP2. I think it was at Monaco that it really started. I was hanging around with Nicholas Todt, who was his manager and also a part owner/manager of the ART GP2 team. So our friendship built up from there.

We went to the Amber Lounge party and we went to dinner a couple of nights, so we got along. We had great respect for each other. We were friends. But like a lot of things in Formula One, things changed as time went by. He was in a different kind of mood later in the year. Things were not going as well for Felipe as they were for me and I think it may have been hard for him to remain happy with the situation. It seemed it was hard for him to keep smiling. But still we get on: he is a good, fun guy and we can joke around together.

After Barcelona, my dad kept me working, like always, and I just got back to basics. The next race was Monaco, my favourite, a place I loved and a circuit where I had always been a winner. I fancied my chances, but I was keeping it to myself. I had had a fantastic race there the previous year in GP2. I loved it, and there is no doubt it is the race every driver wants to win more than any other. There is not one race that comes close to it and I know that I have something there: an ability to drive that track quicker than anyone else. It just feels special.

The place looks so great to start with and then there is the whole glamour thing that hangs around it. There were a lot of promotional events and most of them seemed to be on boats. I decided to duck out of most of all that stuff and keep a low profile and focus on the racing. But there were some sponsors' engagements we had to keep. One of them was a publicity thing we did for the Steinmetz diamond company who prepared our helmets with the words 'Monaco 07' embossed on them in diamonds. I really thought that was pretty cool because for years previously I had seen Kimi there, in Monaco, with diamonds on his helmet, and I had wanted to take his spot or race with him. So, to have my own helmet designed – which actually I put quite a lot of work into myself, to make sure it was good this year – and then for it to have diamonds on it . . . well, it was cool.

I also had to go on a boat and stand with this model. She was stunning and I looked around and just thought to myself, 'Here I am in Monaco, and this is something so cool.' I didn't do any other glamour things but I was given a 'bling' ring that weekend by Steinmetz as a gift. But nothing else took place apart from a party I went to at the end, after the Grand Prix. I did not go to the fashion show or anything else (if I had gone to everything I was invited to, I would have been out all the time) but just stayed in my hotel room, relaxing and focusing on my job. If you do not have that commitment and focus at race weekends, then partying and lovely females can be an easy distraction – as well as a pleasurable one! I had enough to do with the team, in the paddock and in the pits. There were people everywhere, like there always are at the Monaco Grand Prix.

I was not on holiday though. I was there for business. My weekend started okay, even if I did have a small crash in practice on Thursday at Ste Devote. It did not affect me mentally at all. It was my first small hiccup of the racing year, but it was cool. I was finding my limits and I knew I would sort it out. I qualified behind Fernando. He was on pole and I was second but with a heavier fuel load. On that circuit you have to be ahead, on the lighter fuel load, because you really cannot overtake. I knew I was already second and so I had to figure out how, mentally, I was going to turn it my way.

It was not a perfect situation for me but nevertheless I did my best considering the circumstances. The team helped us to manage our cars home by telling me to cool my brakes and take it easy with the car and the barriers. My brakes were fine, or so I thought. I knew I could keep pushing so I did. As usual, we were also told to, 'Turn the engine down' so I was turning the engine down, but I felt Fernando was pulling away and I just wanted to keep pushing.

'Just back off five seconds, for Fernando,' the team said.

'What do you mean, keep it to five seconds? I want to win this race. It's not over till I see a flag.'

'No, just turn it down, keep the gap to five seconds,' they said.

It was then I realized that Fernando was going to win the race but I thought to myself I'm going to make sure people know I have the pace and so I stuck behind him to the end. After the race it was evident that my team were not happy, but I said, 'I'm not here to finish second.'

I really wanted to win at Monaco, I felt I had the pace to win but on reflection what the team decided made sense after all. It really is better to finish at Monaco than risk the barriers and a DNF (did not finish). The decision really affected me because I had never had to hold off from racing before. I was leading the World Championship and was driving to win.

Throughout my racing career, if I was quicker than my team-mate, I was quicker. If I wasn't quicker, then I wasn't and could accept the situation but in Monaco I knew I was quicker. I was disappointed I couldn't continue and get the hat-trick of three consecutive wins because I had won the previous two years in GP2 and Formula Three. Monaco is such a great circuit and when you win it is so special: all the feelings that pour out of you, it is all so rewarding.

Ron came to my room after the race in Monaco, sat down with me and tried to cheer me up. But I was already over it. I am someone who can get over issues and move on pretty quickly. I have learned to do that. My dad taught me how to rise above them: not to sulk but to drive myself on. So I was very straight with Ron and, even though he is the boss – my boss – for me it was a bit different because in the relationship that we have it is almost as if he is like a parent, a mentor and a friend, all in one.

'I really wanted to win this race and I had the opportunity and the speed,' I said.

'You know, this is one race,' he said. 'There'll be other races.'

He was right.

I still enjoyed the fact that I came second in my first Monaco Grand Prix and it was really cool to share the moment, down at the podium, with my brother Nic. I learned a lot about Formula One that day and I was determined to make the most of my next opportunity to win. What I did not know was that the chance I wanted was going to come along much quicker than I thought.

CHAPTER *10*

WINNING

'In those final laps I was just trying to control myself.
I wanted to stop the car and jump out and do
cartwheels or something! I just had to keep it going and
it was mine. It was extremely emotional: to get all the
way to Formula One and then to have my first
pole and my first win –
what a weekend!'

I HAD JUST WON THE CANADIAN GRAND PRIX.

My dad stood there in the crowd and, even from the podium, it looked like he had a tear in his eye. There was nobody else in the world I was going to dedicate that first win to – he was the man who put me there. We were a team. We had done it all together from karts to Formula One. And here I was, standing on the top step of the winners' podium at the Gilles Villeneuve Circuit in Montreal.

No wonder he felt emotional. I could feel his pride. His face betrayed everything. He was feeling so good to see that his family could be that successful. But without him, none of it would have been possible. For me, after all that had happened, it felt immensely satisfying. I had done it for my dad, but also for myself.

I was so happy to have proved a lot of people wrong, the people who had expected me to be way slower than Fernando.

Even when I matched him in pre-season testing, they said, 'Yes, but this is testing . . . Don't be surprised if you are half a second slower than him at the first race.'

I knew that would not happen and so did my dad. That was why I gave him such a huge hug after that race and why I dedicated that win to him. He believed in me absolutely; right from the start. It was a special moment. And it was part of a very special two weeks for us in North America. Looking back now, at the end of a rollercoaster of a season for me, I remember so many things. But one thing I recall so well was when I came across the line in Montreal – not in the race, but in qualifying. That, for me, was the coolest feeling.

Qualifying is so tough, so tense, that it is even more rewarding when you cross the line and they tell you over the radio, 'Congratulations Lewis, you are on pole!' I had some pole positions in Formula Three and in Formula Renault, but this was Formula One! And you might be surprised to hear me say this, but getting pole position is almost even better than winning – it really is. As I found out plenty of times this year, if you do not have pole, then you can be stuck.

Formula One drivers rarely make mistakes, so if you are starting from behind one, you know you have a bit of work to do. The further back you are, the more work you have cut out for you. But if you are on pole, you know you stand a good chance in the race – you have a real chance to win.

Yet from arriving in Canada on the Wednesday right through the weekend, I felt calm and focused. In 2001, I had raced at a kart circuit there, in the first round of the World Championship, but apart from that I had never raced in Canada before – unless you count on computer. When you get to the track, all the kerbs are different, the gradient changes are different, the bumps are a problem and so on. All simulators can do is give you an idea of where the corners are and, perhaps, what gears you should be taking.

Luckily, though, the challenge of racing on new tracks has never really bothered me. Even though it looks a simple circuit, Montreal is actually quite demanding physically, and also quite technical, so it took a while to learn in practice on Friday. That was a good day for me, though and we worked very hard to get the car set-up right. I stayed out of the barriers, which is always good – and not that easy on such a dusty track – and when I went back to the hotel that evening I had some time to think about where I could steal the extra time to get pole.

Going into the third practice session on Saturday morning, we had improved the set-up a lot and then in qualifying the car was just so sweet. For my all important final lap, I had a perfect car and a clear run, and, really, all I had to do was just pull it out. The most important thing was that it was a very consistent lap: I did not make any mistakes at all and I got the time. I remember thinking to myself, 'Wow! I qualified pole and I did not put it in the wall!' To go to Canada for the first time and then compete against Fernando and the Ferraris, who were very quick there, and the BMWs and then to set the car up so well with mine and my team's own setting . . . we really dialled it in for that final qualifying run, but I still had to take the chance. I had an opportunity to go out and put it on pole and I grabbed it with both hands.

No matter what happened in the race after that, it had already been a fantastic weekend. I felt like I had taken another big step in my learning curve. It was not that I was surprised: I knew I had it in me to do it. But I was not sure when it would be.

Before that weekend, I really did not think it would be my time. I thought Fernando was extremely quick in Canada and he would probably get the job done, but that was not the case. I knew I had to stay focused and the only way for me to do that was to be fully relaxed that night. So we did not celebrate. We just had a chilled quiet evening: me, my dad and Adam, my trainer. I made sure I got a good night's sleep so I was ready for the race.

I do not know exactly why, but if I am honest about it, I made quite a poor start in Montreal. I am supposed to have a certain amount of revs to get away fast but I went over that amount, then under to try to get it back. I saw Nick Heidfeld getting close, so I had to shut the door and then I saw Fernando fly past.

Obviously, I did not want him coming past me and I thought, 'Oh no, I'm going to lose it here . . .' But luckily for me he just went straight on over the first corner so I was able to continue with my line – and then I got a fantastic exit. It was exciting, all happening so fast, and it was great to get out in front.

The starts in Formula One are so important and so aggressive. It is a long way from GP2, but I felt I learned from that bad start in Canada. You know you have to be cautious, but at the same time you want to keep your spot. It is about finding a balance. You cannot win the race in the first corner, as the old saying goes, but you certainly can lose it. You have to get around that first one and be safe and bring it home. But you have to have your elbows out and defend your position as well.

After the start, it was a fairly simple race in a way because when I came out of the first turn, still in the lead, that was it. It was my opportunity to get away into the distance. And I would have done that, if it were not for the Safety Car coming out four times. Each time, the field bunched up and I had to make sure that I pulled a good gap out from Heidfeld, who was second. Each time the Safety Car came out, I was thinking 'Uh-oh, someone doesn't want you to win this . . .' and that was because each time you re-start racing, your tyres have got cold, your brakes have got cold and it is so easy to go back out and just put it in the wall. That was the real problem: warming up the tyres enough and not making any mistakes. It did not get to me, though. I thought it was a good challenge – and it kept me busy.

In fact, it was not until there were only about five laps left that I realized I was going to win. I was counting down the laps – five, four, three, two, one – and I was thinking, 'Okay, here we go' and each time I was getting slower and slower and trying to stay off the kerbs. My steering was a little bit off towards the end of the race as well and I thought maybe something was wrong. So, I just tried to stay off the kerbs, but other than that, the car was superb all race.

In those final laps I was just trying to control myself. I wanted to stop the car and jump out and do cartwheels or something! I just had to keep it going and it was mine. It was extremely emotional: to get all the way to Formula One and then to have my first pole and my first win – what a weekend! The Canadian fans were brilliant after the race as they had been throughout. I really did feel like I was on another planet. It had been a fantastic day.

I'd had five podiums and felt I had been ready for the win for quite some time. It was just a matter of when and where – and now it had happened. Obviously it was a big stepping stone in my career and in my life. It was also a really positive thing for the team. That victory signalled to them that they could win races with me, not just with Fernando. That was an important psychological breakthrough for me.

And yet, in all the good things that happened for me, there was one bad thing – the big crash involving Robert Kubica. Robert is an old and good friend of mine from our early karting days and it was a real concern when I was told on the radio about his crash. I did not see the accident, but there was a lot of debris on the track when I went past where it had happened. I was not focusing on his car because I was trying not to run over anything, but it looked serious.

Luckily for me, while the Safety Car was out the team told me, 'He's out, he's on his way to hospital, possibly a broken leg but he's okay.' That was important for me. I knew Robert was okay, so, immediately, I could get on with the race and not have the worry that something serious had happened. I did not have time to go and visit him in hospital, because we had to travel the next morning, but I was obviously relieved when it turned out that he was going to be fine. You never want to see anyone hurt in a crash.

As a racing driver, you always know that bad crashes like Robert's may be just a fraction of a second away, but you do not let it affect you. You cannot afford to – it takes energy away and wastes it in a negative way. When I am in the car, I feel great: it is really comfy in there and I am not worried at all. I know that Formula One has done a fantastic job to make safety a number one priority. I think the results of Robert's crash in Canada and mine in Germany, at the European Grand Prix in July, proved that the sport is pretty safe.

You just cannot take anything for granted. Robert's accident was just a reminder of that for everyone. On one of the happiest and most memorable days of my racing career, I was thinking of him and hoping he would make a complete and speedy recovery.

Robert's accident was just about the main talking point after the race, too. So, despite winning my first Grand Prix and feeling great for doing that, I was feeling a bit reflective as well when we left the track after all the podium formalities and media interviews were over. Of course I wanted to celebrate, but there was another race a week later at Indianapolis and my mum, Linda and Nic were back in England, so it just did not feel right to celebrate without them.

One person that I would especially have loved to have been there was my mum. When I spoke to her afterwards by telephone, she was absolutely kicking herself that she did not go to the race. I had offered her the chance but because of work and other family commitments she was unable to be there.

Usually I try to keep my personal life as far away from my racing as possible, so that when I get to the track it is just me, in my world, and no one can affect it. I never once took my girlfriend Jo to work – and if I did take someone, they would have to be way out at the side so I would never even notice.

It has been very difficult for my family and friends to understand this, but that is how I go to work; that is how I focus. Apart from my dad, when my family come to my races they very rarely see me during the weekend because I am so busy and they like to leave me alone to get on with my job. But that weekend in Montreal I really wanted to share the joy with my mum. When I spoke to her after the race, she was so proud of me and also really upset because she regretted missing what was a huge occasion for me.

That night, after winning my first Grand Prix and leading the World Championship, I somehow managed to remain calm and composed and did not go out drinking. We did go to a big barbeque, which was good, and then after that I was up early the next morning to fly to New York. That is the thing with Formula One: it never gives you time to rest on your laurels. I went to New York with my dad and Adam and it was good for all of us to be able to escape and to relax a little bit. It was not my first time visiting New York, but it is not a city I know that well. I was happy to just chill out and look around. I did not go out partying or anything, but did take the chance to have some unhealthy food, some chicken wings, and I was quite happy with that. Through that week, we were focusing on the next race. It is so easy to just go partying and then take a couple of days to recover but it is like cheating yourself – you know you are not going to be at your best for the next race.

So in New York we had a job to do and we knew it. I was lucky, too, because I met up with a good friend, Jeffery Roberts who works for Mercedes-Benz USA, and so we hung out and went to a New York Yankees versus Arizona Diamondbacks baseball game. It was just a cool time. I did get recognized a couple of times, but only by tourists from Europe and that was nice. None of the Americans noticed me at all. I was able to walk around as free as everyone else, which helped me to chill. One thing that did stop me relaxing as much as I would have liked, though, was the two hundred or so text messages I got from friends back home, all saying 'Well done!' I was not going to start complaining about that, though!

From New York, I went to Washington DC and then to Indianapolis for the United States Grand Prix. The team had arranged a couple of sponsor appearances for me in New York and Washington, so I never really felt I had stopped work completely. Then we were on our way to 'The Brickyard' and another race weekend. The flight from Washington kept getting delayed. It went from four o'clock in the afternoon to eight o'clock that evening, half an hour at a time, then eventually it was cancelled at nine. So we ended up staying in a hotel and luckily we managed to get a flight to Indy on the Thursday morning.

When I got to the track, I literally went straight into the official pre-race media conference, which is held with four or five drivers on the Thursday prior to a race. I had to answer questions about everything from the history of the circuit to me and Fernando and comparisons between me and Tiger Woods. It was an intensive session.

Tiger Woods is one of the greatest golfers ever and has completely changed the way that his sport is perceived by millions of people. I was just a rookie driver who had won my first Grand Prix only a few days earlier – and I am certainly no threat to him as a golfer! Having said that, I knew where the Tiger Woods comparison questions were heading, so I just answered them in the way I always did. I have said already that, for me, race is not an issue at all so I was comfortable just handling all the questions from the American reporters and they seemed pretty happy with the answers.

Of course, I think Tiger Woods is a sensational athlete and it is an honour to be compared to someone like him. But I do not want to be the Tiger Woods of motor racing – just being the Lewis Hamilton of motor racing will be cool enough for me. I am completely different to Tiger Woods, but if I can have a similar impact on Formula One to that which he has had on golf, then I will be delighted. Basically, I just tried to be honest and polite and they all looked satisfied with that. Anyway, I am terrible at golf. I can hit the ball, but not very consistently, and I refuse to have lessons because I have watched my dad's friend Terry having lessons and his game is still worse than mine although he'd tell you different! Having said that, if I met Tiger Woods I would be happy to have lessons from him!

There was another thing, though, that cropped up in that first press conference in Indianapolis – it was the first time that Fernando made comments about the team helping me more than him. I found it strange when he said that, especially after what happened to me in Monaco. As far as I was aware and concerned, the team and everything else was completely fair and equal for us both. Obviously, I already had a great relationship with all the guys because I had been to the team fitness and team building week in Finland with them earlier in the year. And I guess because Fernando is Spanish and I am English, he might have felt that there was something else going on but there was nothing.

I doubt very much that Fernando expected me to do as well as I did. Coming into the team as a two-time World Champion, he had not really been challenged too closely before. I do not believe he expected a rookie to challenge him so strongly, let alone beat him, but it was just racing. I was just there doing my best and I was, as I often said, very much living the dream. Certain things that came with my success were even surprising me.

The whole time I was in Montreal and then in Indianapolis there was a lot of interest shown in me by the media and also by a lot of fans out there. I was really shocked to see that there was so much support. When you are just a newcomer you simply do not think about, or expect to see, any support in a country you do not really know. So when you get there and you see that you have fans, it is a real shock to the system. In Indianapolis, especially, I got a lot of support from the Americans: they were extremely nice people and it was good to meet so many of them. I think that because I had been in New York, I did not really appreciate the level of interest that was developing. I was told by people at home that I was on the front page of all the newspapers in the UK on the Monday after the Canada race, which was pretty awesome. But other than that, I really had no feel for what had gone on around the world. I actually think that was a good thing because I was able to relax for a little while before the Indianapolis race.

When we got to Indy, I was lucky enough to meet up with Pharrell Williams, one of my own heroes from the music world, and that helped me stay cool. Things just worked out nicely. Pharrell was the American solo rapper who founded the band N*E*R*D and I have been a big fan of his for years and years. We had spoken on the phone a few times before, but I finally met him at Indianapolis. He was the first real top dog celebrity that I had met and, to me, he is a pretty big star, especially in the music that I am into. I buy his albums and, for me, this is a cool cat. He came to the race as my guest. We had dinner with him, I got to know him better and our friendship grew from there. We hooked up and we were like boys, you know, and got on really well. Like all the Americans I met, he was really supportive towards me that weekend.

That helped me a lot as I also really wanted to do well at Indianapolis because another of my friends, Dario Franchitti, had just won the Indy 500 there. Despite his name, Dario is a Scot so I did not want to be the one to let the Brits down that weekend – although I hardly needed the extra motivation, given the championship positions and the way my season had gone up to that point. On top of that, you always want to perform your best at somewhere like Indy because it is such a legendary venue. I think a lot of people in Formula One were sad to see it drop off the calendar after that race and I definitely was one of them.

Even in the few days that had passed since the Canadian race, the team had been working hard on the car for America. There is no let-up, even after a win. It is the McLaren and Mercedes-Benz way. As always, they did a good job and the car was sweet again when I went out to learn my second new circuit inside a week. I knew roughly where the corners were, apart from that, though, I did not know what to expect so I just went about my job with an open mind and tried to repeat what I had done in Montreal. And, luckily for me, it worked again.

The pole at Indianapolis was even more satisfying than in Canada. Fernando is usually very quick at Indy and we were on equal fuel loads for qualifying. I did a very, very good lap and got pole position. Again, as in Canada, I remember those seconds when I went across the finish line and then I was just waiting, hoping, thinking, 'Okay, Lewis, I put everything I had into that lap; did I get it?' And then they came across on the radio and I heard: 'Nice job Lewis, you're pole.' Phwoooooar! As I said before, it is an amazing feeling. And I do not think that sort of feeling will ever fade. When the team told me I had P1 over my radio, I was screaming in my helmet, and through the whole warm-down lap I was just ecstatic.

It was quite a surprise, to be honest, because going into qualifying, we had not found the optimal set-up and I knew that Fernando was going to be extremely quick. All through qualifying at Indy, I was finding bits of time through my driving and I saw certain places where I could find even more. Going into my qualifying laps in Q3, the car felt very good. I made certain adjustments on my steering wheel and the balance was very good and I managed to get a very clear lap. Once again, I just had to pull it all out and my last two last laps in Q3 were spot on. I think I just beat my best lap at the end and I had two laps that were good enough for pole. As I got out of the car, I remember looking around at the crowd and seeing a lot of British flags and flags with my name on.

I could see outside my garage, over in the grandstands, that someone had a Vodafone McLaren Mercedes sign with 'Lewis' on it. That was great to see. That kind of thing gives me a real buzz.

I had learned from my poor start in Montreal and I got away cleanly in Indianapolis. From there, the race went smoothly. I was cruising, really, in the lead on my own. I had pulled out a really nice gap and Fernando was maybe a couple of seconds behind me. But I looked at the computer data at the end of the race and from being right behind me he was able to gain three or four tenths of a second a lap. I was pulling him along basically, so he was able to keep with me. Obviously he was in my slipstream the whole time so he could always catch me down the straight and so whatever I gained on the infield I would lose on the straight.

After the first pit stops, I got held up by a back-marker and Fernando got a good run up to the last corner. He was right up my tail and he had an opportunity, but there was no way I was letting him past. At one point, we did battle almost literally wheel-to-wheel, but he was not coming past. I am no pushover – if anything, I am one of the hardest drivers to overtake, that is for sure. I know how to protect my position at all times fair and square. But on that straight I knew I had to make sure that I made one move and made it stick. So I moved into the inside. As long as I braked late, he would stay behind. I managed that, but then he was on me for the next few corners before I was able to break away again. It was very, very tough racing. He fought well, but at the end I managed to pull out a gap and was able to control the rest of the race.

The crowd were a big help. I was told there were over 100,000 people at the circuit and I got a lot of energy from that. The big support and all the British flags out there were fantastic for me but the last few laps were draining. It just seemed to take so long. The team came on the radio and said, 'Fifteen laps' and I said, 'Okay' and those fifteen laps just seemed a lifetime. It was very hot and it is quite draining when you are out in the lead, trying to maintain it, not to push too hard, not to damage the car. What a dream day that was again. Another victory – and scenes of jubilation all around me again. I had not realized it was Father's Day in America. Someone told me, but I had already dedicated the last race to my dad and had already planned to dedicate this one to Nic. I do not think he minded too much; he seemed pretty happy when I saw him afterwards, anyway.

Looking back on that whole North America trip, it was just amazing. It was extremely intense, but I thoroughly enjoyed every minute of it. The people were great and I was treated well everywhere: Montreal, New York, Indianapolis. To go to Canada and Indianapolis for the first time and have the best two races of my life was just incredible. I felt so proud and so honoured because, before the season, I absolutely could not have imagined it. I came into the season with a very open mind and was realistic about the fact that I was a rookie who had a lot to learn. I was in one of the best cars with one of the best drivers in my team to compare myself to. But I just tried to approach every race exactly the same, do the same things and try to improve. I knew there would be some hard times, but that was inevitable.

It was great to leave America in the lead, but with ten races left in the season it was way too early to consider winning the championship. Even after two wins in a row, I knew I could not win every race and that the most important thing was to stay consistent. I was in the lead by ten points, but there was no reason to think about it. I just continued enjoying it all. The moment you start to think about the championship is the moment you start losing.

Though I did not get carried away, the North America trip was definitely a real boost to my confidence. Any positive thing that happens in my life has that effect, but you have a measure: you can get a 1 per cent boost or a 100 per cent boost. A 100 per cent boost is very rare. And in North America I got two.

CHAPTER

SILVERSTONE

'It did take some getting used to – hanging out with P. Diddy, calling him Sean and having all these famous people's numbers on my phone. I went to sit with Pharrell. I almost had to pinch myself! There I was, just a few days away from the biggest race of my life and at a private dinner with P. Diddy and Pharrell Williams. It was that kind of week.'

WHEN I CAME BACK TO EUROPE after those wonderful weeks in North America, my life was totally flipped upside down. I was on a completely different planet. All the attention was something really new to me. From being virtually unknown at the start of the year, I had become someone everyone recognized. People wanted to know all about me, not just my views on racing, but on girls, music, religion and anything else they thought about.

I knew I had been attracting a lot of attention in America, but when I was told that 20,000 people had turned up to see me drive at the pre-British Grand Prix test at Silverstone, it made me stop and think, 'Wow!' This was not for the British Grand Prix, not for the race, nor for qualifying and not even for practice. The Grand Prix was weeks away. I have never been the kind of person who expects a crowd to follow me around so I did not really believe they were there for me but everyone told me they were.

What a great feeling that was! Sadly I was not at the test and so could not fulfil the fans' hopes of seeing me on the circuit. The big crowd for that test did make me stop and think just what was happening. I started to think, if it is this crazy now, then what about the actual British Grand Prix itself, my home race, a few weeks later at Silverstone?

Before tackling the British weekend, we had to go to France, to Magny-Cours where, after all the euphoria of Montreal and Indianapolis, it was a bit of a disappointment for me personally. I thought we were pretty steady in qualifying. I could have got pole again if I had not made a minor mistake on my final lap. But I was on the front row with Felipe Massa. Felipe is one of the drivers that I got on well with and I felt we had developed a decent level of trust. We all want to beat each other. As a rookie, I knew I had to earn the respect of the other drivers. Nothing comes easy in Formula One. In the French Grand Prix at Magny-Cours, my start was poor and, to be honest, I really did not know why. All I saw was Kimi Räikkönen come flying past me in his Ferrari. He obviously got a good start. I do not like being overtaken, and it was the first time that it had happened on the track in Formula One. After that, I tried to stay as close to Kimi as possible. I thought I was quicker than him in the first part of the race, but sometimes in Formula One you have to be seconds faster to pass someone, so I never really had a chance.

The Ferraris were very quick that weekend, but overall I was happy with my third place and six more championship points. As always, I knew that consistency was the most important thing and I could not have been happier than to have delivered my eighth podium finish in a row. Well, that is, unless we were faster than the Ferrari and could have won the race! Finishing on the podium is always great, but I could not deny that after the two previous races the result that day was not quite as special to me. I needed to remind myself that to finish third in a Grand Prix, any Grand Prix anywhere, beaten only by two Ferraris, is still a cool thing. Plan A is to beat everyone. Plan B is to finish ahead of your team-mate. If Plan A does not work, at least you can feel some satisfaction if you succeed with Plan B. But if Plan B fails, well then you think 'Shoot . . .'

After that race someone told me that Fernando, who finished seventh, said he was happy that the Ferraris had beaten me so I did not take maximum points. I can understand that. His Plan B had failed and he was looking for any consolation. At the time, I did not even know he had said this, but it would not have worried me if I had known. He had begun to be less cooperative as I started winning races. It is not a case of wishing anything bad on anyone, but if your rival does not take as many points as he could have done, then that is a good thing for you. Generally though, I do not focus on anyone else in a race weekend but rather on my own performance.

If Magny-Cours was a bit of a dull race on a hot weekend in the middle of France, Silverstone was amazing. Wow! The amount of people that were there, so many wearing my cap or my McLaren top – it was really something else. The year before, in GP2, I had had a huge reception from the crowds that were there to watch Formula One, but who also came to support and cheer me on. I remember hoping that the next time I went to Silverstone I would be at the front and that everyone would be again cheering me on and that I would be able to do them proud. And here I was! I was just floating the whole week. I was buzzing, not really knowing what to expect, but loving it. I had a few sponsor events in the week running up to the race and loads of other appearances so it was quite intense and, thinking about it now, it was probably the hardest place to stay focused on my job in that way. You try to manage your time and to maximize the days you have off, but the marketing department have got their jobs to do and around the time of the races at Magny-Cours and Silverstone, I did not get much time to myself.

Before the British race, I went to a karting event in Milton Keynes organized by Vodafone which I really enjoyed. I liked being able to make the young drivers happy and give them some of my time in the hope that it would inspire them. I thought it was important that I give them my perspective on how I got where I am and encourage them to follow their own ambitions and do their best to make them come true. Everyone has a dream.

At one of these events, I was asked which former driver I would most like to race against and I went for Michael Schumacher. I got a laugh by saying I was disappointed that he had bailed out the year I got to Formula One. Of course, I was joking, but there was a bit of truth in it. I have already said that I do not agree with some of his controversial moves, but as a competitor there was nobody better and I would have loved to race against him. He was also a great professional off the track and I have tried to copy the way people like him manage with everything, especially in really busy weeks like that one I had before Silverstone. It is mostly mental energy that you are losing; you must try not to empty 'the bottle' of your own energy to keep everyone else happy. It is not always easy to keep a smile on – or make sure you say the right things. It is probably one of the trickiest parts of the job, but you just have to get on with it.

Whenever something seems potentially complicated, I just simplify it so I can deal with it. If someone writes, or says, something about you, what difference does it really make? If it is positive, it is all good energy, and if it is negative you block it out. I just put all the attention in a sieve, drain away all the crap and then use the good stuff.

It was not all hard work, however, as I did take a bit of time out to relax before going up to Silverstone. After meeting Pharrell in Indianapolis, I got a chance to meet another music star I had looked up to for a long time – P. Diddy. He was in London and I was invited to meet him. Unfortunately, I was in the middle of such an intense week that it was impossible for me to take up his invitation. I wanted to focus on my weekend, but at the same time I absolutely love his music and wanted to meet him and I hoped I would get another chance at some other time.

I am mostly into hip-hop, R'n'B and reggae, but I am very open-minded. I really love jazz, I like some classical music and I love listening to blues. I am probably biggest on reggae, jazz and blues at the moment. I really admire musicians who are creative in their work, can read music and play instruments with their heart and soul. Most R'n'B and hip-hop is created on computer. You still have to be very talented to have an ear for that sort of thing; it is just a different kind of production and as I play the guitar myself, I'm into musicians who play instruments. I admit I do not play fantastically well and I really wish I could, but I enjoy it. It makes me look at people who play way better than me and really respect them for their talent and work. I try to take my guitar to every race and I miss it badly if I forget it or something happens to prevent me playing it. At Monza, for example, I lost the key to the guitar case on the plane on the way over. Luckily, we found it on the way back, but I missed it that weekend. I could have cracked the case open but didn't want to damage it.

I soon got another opportunity to meet P. Diddy when he invited me to another function he was holding in London. I thought, 'You never know when you're going to have that kind of opportunity again' and I decided to go and I am really glad that I did. We were told that everyone had to be there, and sitting down, by eight o'clock. But I was delayed returning from a sponsors' event and I arrived late at nine o'clock and for some reason people were still standing. As soon as I arrived, P. Diddy came over and talked to me – and then people started to sit down. So, not only was I there with all these guests waiting, but when we go to sit down, I am on P. Diddy's table. And not just that – I am sitting next to him, too. How cool was that? He was some dude.

What was he like? Well, he was really very down to earth. He was talking about his life, talking about normal stuff. He was asking me things about racing and it was clear he did not understand too much about a Formula One car. So, he was like, 'When you do this, how does the car feel? What's this? What's that? Tell me about pit stops . . .' So, basically, I just filled him in on what happens on a race weekend. Then we talked about music and the next track he is going to release. He said, 'Yeah, my next album's gonna be crazy, something completely different.' And I am sitting there going, 'Yeah, yeah, man . . . I'll make sure I get it!'

But it was an incredibly cool evening and we had a good meal. Afterwards, people started going round and talking. Quite a few people came up and asked me for my phone number, which was strange for me, but I kind of liked it. It did take some getting used to – hanging out with P. Diddy, calling him Sean and having all these famous people's numbers on my phone. I went to sit with Pharrell and I almost had to pinch myself! There I was, just a few days away from the biggest race of my life, and I was at a private dinner with P. Diddy and Pharrell Williams. How cool was that! It was that kind of week.

The next day some of the newspapers made out that I was with a certain young lady and also that I was becoming familiar with drinking champagne but they got that all wrong. I was not with the lady in question and I don't drink during the racing season. I was on an evening out with P. Diddy and Pharrell, it was all completely normal and innocent. I have been brought up to be a gentleman at all times.

Everywhere I went that Silverstone week, there were all these expectations. I was not really sure exactly how many people were going to be there, but I had all these different events to do and I was thinking, 'I know there will be a lot of people there because this is my home country and the people here support me.' That level of support meant there was a lot of pressure all weekend. There is nothing worse, in terms of that kind of pressure of expectation, than to be sitting in your car in the garage and to know that your team-mate is ahead of you. For me, it translated as, 'The Spanish guy is ahead of you and you're in front of the British crowd at home at Silverstone!' It was like feeling embarrassed in front of your family. You know that feeling – you do not want to be embarrassed in front of them. Well, I felt that way about the whole country. So, I worked as hard as I could and, in qualifying at least, I came out on top. I did not get distracted although there was a lot of potential for it. As always, the most pressure came from myself. It has always been that way.

Silverstone is a breathtaking circuit. It has always been one of my favourites. It has a lot of high-speed corners, so it is very physically demanding but extremely technical as well. That, combined with the history of the place and the fans, makes it a special place for me. Even in practice, there were a lot of people there and a lot of British flags all round the track. Everything went okay, but I have to admit I never felt completely comfortable with the car. I chose a different rear-end set-up to Fernando and in hindsight that was probably a mistake. The Ferraris were faster than us, but as always I was still confident we could respond and do it going into qualifying. As it turned out, I was right.

That Saturday at Silverstone was an awesome day, one of my best memories of the whole year. It is difficult to put it into words: hot weather, perfect conditions that you can have in England in the summer, 80,000 fans – everything was perfect, including my final qualifying lap. It went really well and I got that amazing pole position feeling again. This time I was just faster than Kimi's Ferrari and Fernando was third. I know I am repeating it, but when you are in the car and you know you are on the last lap in a qualifying session, you know the slightest mistake means you lose it. So you are sitting on a knife edge all the way round and somehow you put it all together. That is what happened for me. It was a phenomenal feeling. When you find out you got the time you needed, it really is amazing.

It is even better when you have got that sort of pressure on you – I could see so many fans everywhere. It was fantastic to see all the support I had behind me. It was almost unreal. It is difficult to say how much time it gives you, but it definitely helps. I felt a huge energy boost at Silverstone that afternoon.

At most races, there will be pockets of supporters here and there, but at Silverstone it was whole grandstands. I could not believe how many people were there on Saturday. When I pulled out the lap and came across the line I could see the reaction of the fans and it was a very, very good feeling. Inside the car, I was screaming my head off. I nearly lost my voice. I could hear the crowd going crazy and I was screaming just as loud as them! I was not shouting into my radio – I would not do that to the team – but just shouting to myself. I did it in Canada too, the whole way round the circuit after I won that race. I am surprised my voice stood up to all that! Trust me, it is a long, long lap when you are sitting in top gear and cruising round, but it is great to soak it all up. The fans are an important part of the event and provide everyone with inspiration and motivation.

During the Formula One Drivers' Parade, I like to spot as many different people that have come to support me and I try to make eye contact with them. It is obviously very difficult when you are standing on the back of a moving truck, but I try to point and let them know that I have noticed them because I do really appreciate it. Even if it is just one dude being out there, I appreciate him being that one dude and giving me his support.

The race was interesting, but a bit of a struggle for me. The crowd helped me through in the end. It was all pretty amazing on the grid and before the start – there were so many celebrities around, but I tried to just ignore any distractions and do my own routine. David and Victoria Beckham were there and it was cool to meet them. But my mind was on the job. We all have different ways of preparing for something like that. Before the race, before we get to the grid, I spend time in my room switching off, not wasting my energy. I just lie down, totally still, relaxing, bringing my heart-rate down. It was the same as usual at Silverstone. I always get out of the car, once we are on the grid, before the race starts. I do not want to sit in there and relax. It is so comfortable in the seat when you are strapped in that you could easily go to sleep. It is so warm and you just feel very cosy. They put the parasol or umbrella up and you nearly shut off. You can easily enter a too-relaxed frame of mind. It is almost like lying in bed. That is why I get out and keep myself moving.

It started off pretty nicely. I got away well, which was important, but when I tried to pull away from Kimi he was extremely quick and then towards the end of my opening stint my tyres started deteriorating badly. Kimi got quite close and then, when I went in for my first pit stop, I made a mistake. I tried to pull away too soon. I thought that the pit crew had started to lift the 'lollipop', a sign on a stick that they put in front of you when you are stopped so you can read the team instructions easily. I thought I saw the lollipop move a little bit, but I was wrong. And, at the same time, I let the clutch out too soon. You try to be as quick as you can when the lollipop goes up because it is so important to get away quickly and rejoin the race. I tried to anticipate it and I was too early. Then I had to stop again and it was all a bit of a mess. I do not know how many seconds I lost through that, but it was an individual mistake by me and cost me quite a bit of valuable time. It also let Kimi and Fernando get past me. After that I just had to try to push, but I struggled with the balance of the car.

Through the whole weekend, I had been struggling to find the perfect balance. Obviously qualifying went well, but in the race we lacked a little bit of speed. Kimi was too quick and I could have ended up finishing behind Felipe as well, if he had not had to start from the back of the grid after stalling at the start.

I never gave up though. I just kept on pushing because you never know what is going to happen. The guys in front could have come together and had an accident. They could have got caught out behind back-markers and if that happened I wanted to be there. Sometimes, I could see people ahead and I did not know exactly who it was. I thought maybe they would be getting close to back-markers and I thought, 'This is my opportunity to keep pushing because I might get close.' Even when the team told me to turn the engine down, to save it for the next race, I would not give up. My car was getting slower, but I tried to push even harder to compensate for the engine. In the end, I was third behind Kimi and Fernando. It was good, really, considering the car had not been too great. And, without the support I had from the crowd, it would have been a much harder race. I knew the fans were with me all the way and hopefully next time I can go all the way and really give them something to shout about.

I learned a good lesson from the race. I am not one of those people who blame the equipment. In fact, I blame the way I set my equipment up because that is the only way something can go wrong unless something fails – and nothing failed that weekend. I set the car up and we did not have the pace of the Ferraris. I have to take the blame for that. I did not get the best setting to optimize the car and I made a mistake at the pit stop. Both of those things are on me. We worked really hard, but I chose the wrong rear end in the first place and that caused problems. On the positive side, I came away with a ninth consecutive podium and my lap times were pretty consistent all weekend. Being on pole, I felt quite strongly that I could have had a better result, but I think most people were happy enough with my third place. To go to your first home Grand Prix and still get a podium is alright – you have to look on the bright side.

CHAPTER  **12**

ADVERSITY

'The next thing I remember was the tyre blew and I was off heading for the tyre wall which I knew was going to hurt because I was going forwards, not sideways or backwards ... I had pretty much no support at all, just my seatbelts. I tried to brace myself and make sure I was ready for the impact, which you never can be, and it hurt like ... Well, it hurt a lot!'

I WAS OPERATING ON SUCH A HIGH all the way through the British Grand Prix week that I could not identify what was really going on. I was feeling a bit fatigued and in the run-up to the next race – the European Grand Prix at the Nürburgring in Germany – I started to feel unwell. I had a virus and felt as if I had a touch of some kind of flu. We had such a hectic programme through early July, with the back-to-back races in France and at Silverstone, that there had not been enough time to rest.

After nine consecutive podium finishes, leading the World Championship and suddenly being fêted everywhere, I was experiencing life as I had never done before. It was all new, every day really. I was still enjoying everything, but I was aware that it was getting harder and harder to maintain my performance levels and my consistency. In the first few races,

I just went out and pushed to the limit. But as the season went by, the expectations changed and I felt a different kind of responsibility for the points I was aiming to win for myself and for the team.

As always, in the middle of the European part of the season, in the high summer, there were a lot of engagements to do for sponsors, the team and partners. I enjoy them, and I understand how important they are, but they take a huge amount of time and energy and you just have to learn to manage it somehow. I had done nine races and I had been on the podium at every single one, an amazing record that I would never in a million years have dreamt of achieving before the season began. So I had no reason to worry about anything going into the Nürburgring, especially as it is a circuit I like and where I'd had good results in the past. I had a great weekend there in 2006 in GP2 where I had my first double win of the year. And in 2005 I also won there in Formula Three with ASM, a team that was powered by Mercedes-Benz engines. I had great support from the crowd and I could remember how wonderful that felt. So I had good vibes about the coming race even though I was feeling a bit under the weather.

I was looking forward to driving a McLaren Mercedes-Benz in front of that crowd again and I also felt encouraged by a good performance at the Spa-Francorchamps test. The car felt better there than it had all season and I got a boost from that. I knew the Nürburgring track pretty well, too, so I had a decent understanding of how the car should be set up, and that traction was important for the exit from the slow corners and that I needed good balance especially in the first sector of the circuit. I had prepared properly and by the Thursday before that race weekend, I was feeling a lot better than I had done earlier in the week.

That Thursday was quite a busy day, as there had been a few appearances and we had done a karting event for Voda-fone. Also, I was one of the drivers asked to attend the pre-race press conference, so I had plenty to pack in. I remember how much I enjoyed the karting with a group of youngsters and how committed they were. I was impressed. They were so young and yet so focused and so fast. I was asked if that reminded me of myself at that age, and I said yes. I was impressed by their attitude and their determination.

It was cold and wet at the Nürburgring – someone said it was typical English weather but actually it was much worse than we normally get in England. And it is worth saying, too, that the wet weather seems to just hang in the trees and all around in the hills and valleys at the Nürburgring because the track is up in the Eifel mountains. It is just that kind of place. Stunning.

One of the things that had been cropping up again and again by that stage of the season was a host of questions about the McLaren team – about the Ferrari controversy. It had started before Silverstone and I had put it out of my mind. I really knew nothing about it at all, though later on in the season it was clear that it really mattered a lot and had a huge effect on our championship hopes. But at the time of the European Grand Prix, I was not too bothered and only focused on my job.

I felt confident about myself, my driving, and the integrity of the team and so I felt that I had nothing to worry about. I had every faith in them. I knew what McLaren had done over the years and I knew the people. I just could not believe that anything negative would happen – it did not seem possible. I was more interested in my car and the set-up and performance, to be honest. I was not into the politics of Formula One; all I wanted to do was go fast and try to win. We did not manage to have the right set-up at Silverstone and going into the Nürburgring weekend I was hoping for a better result.

The Spa test had gone well for me. I drove on a nice clear day with no rain – I think everyone else had rain after I had left. That test left me feeling a lot better. When you drive a car that you are comfortable with, it is just a pleasure. So I enjoyed testing in Belgium and I took the confidence with me into Friday's practice at the Nürburgring. We focused, as always, on tyre evaluation and general set-up work, but it was affected a bit by the wet weather. Despite that, I found a good balance early on. I felt pretty happy with the car. We had introduced some aerodynamic changes for the weekend. I went out on the drying track to gain experience, thinking I had not done a lot of running in those conditions in a Formula One car. It was just in case we had more rain and similar weather – you have to try to prepare for everything.

In qualifying on the Saturday, I felt pretty quick and thought I was on top of things. We got to Q3 and it was looking very good. I started my qualifying lap, still feeling like there was a possibility of me taking pole. I got to a corner – I think it was turn eight – and I went off, but I had already felt something going just after turn seven. I sort of shrugged it off as nothing. The next thing I remember was the tyre blew and I was off heading for the tyre wall which I knew was going to hurt because I was going forwards, not sideways or backwards. There was nothing I could do. I was a passenger and a huge crash was about to happen. I had pretty much no support at all, just my seatbelts. I tried to brace myself and make sure I was ready for the impact, which you never can be, and it hurt like . . . Well, it hurt a lot! It was not to be the last time that my tyres were the cause of a major incident for me but this was the worst.

In a situation like that you have no time to think or do anything except react in an instinctive way, trying to do the right things you've been taught. It is one thing to be trained to brace yourself and another to do it when your car is hurtling into a wall of tyres at 150 mph and you are out of control. I was still conscious when the impact came and it shook me up badly.

It was really one of the most painful crashes I have ever had. My chest and my legs felt it. I think I hit my legs on the side of the cockpit and also my chest somewhere hard because my head went so far forward. It was a bad one and it is difficult

to describe. I damaged all the top muscles of my chest and I rup-
tured one of the ligaments in between my ribs. I thought I had
broken my right leg and broken a rib because of the pain, but,
eventually, I calmed down and thought 'Let's get outta here!' I
pulled myself out of the car and tried walking and my right leg
hurt so much that I fell down on the ground. It must have been
all the adrenaline and everything else that kept me going until
that point. Then the medical team came and took control.

The only problem was me. Sometimes you just feel that
you do not want to be hurt and taken away. You just want to
get back in the car again and ignore the pain. So I said,
'Shoot, oh no! I'm okay . . . I know I'm okay and I want it.'
My first thought when I was put on a stretcher was, 'I hope I
can get back to the garage in time to get out in the spare car.'
I wanted to go back out, I wanted to qualify. I asked the
medical team if I could get back to the garage to the spare car
and they were like, 'There's no way you're getting back in
there!' It was not what I wanted to hear. I just wanted to get
back out and finish the lap but soon realized it was not going
to happen.

They told me qualifying was nearly over. The whole time
they were talking, the same thoughts kept going through my
mind: 'How and when can I get back in the car? All I want to
do is race tomorrow!' I could not take in what was going on. I
was worried where I would start on the grid if I started at all.

After a full check-up back at the medical centre, I
was flown to the local hospital. The doctors put me through a

thorough medical including a body scan plus numerous tests. It was a very worrying time, it was like, 'Jeez, this doctor could say, "No, No, he cannot race tomorrow,"' like what happened to Robert Kubica in Indy. And if he said that, it would have been disastrous. I'd be out of the race.

Fortunately, after all the tests the doctor was satisfied that I was just badly bruised and wanted to wait until the next morning before giving his decision whether I would be allowed to take the grid for the race.

I was very, very sore the next day, but I wanted to do the race. People asked me: 'How are you?' I was like, 'No I'm fine, I'm fine.' Luckily, I had slept well overnight, even with the injuries. I took a few painkillers and they helped me a lot, and in any case I have almost never had any problems with sleeping.

My crash in qualifying meant that the session was red-flagged. The tyre blowout had been caused by a wheel gun failure – the right front wheel had not been fixed on properly. It was one of those things. In the pits the wheel gun sounded like it had fully tightened the wheel nut and it felt right but in fact it had only delivered about half the torque pressure necessary to lock the wheel. Nobody wants that kind of accident, but you have to focus on what lies ahead – not on the past. I had a big bruise to remind me of the pain. I had to have a medical check-up on the race morning with the FIA medical delegate, Dr Gary Hartstein, and the chief medical officer of the event, Dr Klaus Zerbian. They said I was fine to race and, for me, that was fantastic news. The only problem now was that I was back in tenth place on the grid, on the fifth row with Ralf Schumacher in his Toyota. The main thing, however, was that I would be racing. So, once again, I just remained positive and felt sure that I could do a good job.

Race day started in damp conditions. Bad weather was expected but it started raining sooner than we thought. Fortunately, I got the best start I had all year! I was up to sixth after the first turn and then something happened that now, with hindsight, I regret because it cost me dearly later on. Robert Kubica and Nick Heidfeld, who were BMW team-mates, collided. I saw the two BMWs starting to slide backwards and, in that instant, decided that I was going to go to the right and pass them on the outside. That was where the grip was and where I wanted to move. Just as I was on the outside, they collided and then Robert was rolling backwards. He had spun. I could only hope his car would not touch mine, but it did. His rear wing, or the diffuser, clipped my left rear tyre. It left me with a puncture and, from then on, everything became more and more difficult. Sometimes, things just happen. I was just not meant to win that race.

After all my previous good luck, it was extraordinary in a different kind of way. I had a puncture and had to pit. I guess in a way it was a bit lucky for me because the team took advantage of that opportunity and fitted rain tyres. The rain was torrential by now and it was so slippery that I was aquaplaning, and then I went off at turn one. Maybe I was pushing too hard

‘ My first HUGO BOSS
photoshoot 2004. ’

Dicing with Fernando at the Canadian Grand Prix.

Right A dream come true – my first Formula One win, Montreal, Canada, 10 June 2007.

Above The sweetest feeling – the moment I crossed the line.

Above Reaching out to my dad after my first win.

THE TIMES

Monday June 11 2007 timesonline.co.uk No 69035   65p

Eat out from £15
Quaglino's ● Savoy Grill Details times2

Nadal triumphs
Sport, pages 74, 75

Unmarried couples get equal rights on 'divorce'

▶ New legal remedies for 4 million cohabitees

▶ Children and careers will be the key factors

Frances Gibb Legal Editor

Cohabiting partners who split up are to get similar rights to divorcing couples under plans to be outlined next month, *The Times* has learnt.

Unmarried women and men will be able to make claims against their partners to demand lump-sum payments, a share of property, regular maintenance or a share of the partner's pension when they separate. They will also be able to claim against their partners for loss of earnings if they gave up a career to look after children.

The reforms are to be published by the Law Commission, the Government's law reform body. It is expected to drop any proposal for a time stipulation, so that only couples who had lived together for, say, two years could bring a claim, or any bar on childless couples.

Plans that would have made it harder for the partner who stays at home to bring a claim have also been dropped. Courts will no longer have to be satisfied that the

unmarried couple jointly decided that one of them should give up their career and stay at home and that the decision was not made just by one of them.

At present, cohabiting partners have no financial rights if their relationship breaks down, regardless of how long they have lived together. If there are children in the relationship, the partner who has residency will get child maintenance but can make no other claim.

The proposed reforms will offer legal remedies to up to two million cohabiting couples.

Ministers have indicated that they favour reform, but there is no definite slot for legislation. However, there is mounting pressure for unmarried couples to have greater legal recognition: in April the House of Lords ruled that, if an unmarried couple owned a house in joint names, the assumption should be that they owned it in equal shares.

The Law Commission reforms aim to strike a delicate balance: they seek to give cohabitees who break up protection similar to those far divorcing couples, but to stop short of automatic rights to a financial share. This means that the courts would have the same

Continued on page 4, col 2

We don't do drugs
87% of teenagers say no, times2

King of the road and a new British hero

Lewis Hamilton raced to a first Grand Prix win. News, page 8 Sport, pages 70-86

Scramble to opt out threatens EU summit

Prospects of a deal on the future of Europe at Tony Blair's final summit are threatened by fears that a rash of demands for opt-outs from EU laws will turn the negotiations into a farce. Ministers are expecting several countries to call for exclusions from legislation they find unacceptable. News, page 2

Cleaning up Abuja

The police and politicians of the Nigerian capital are cutting out the backhanders and cleaning up their collective act in an effort to win the race against Glasgow and secure the 2014 Commonwealth Games. World Focus, page 35

Slimline sweeties

A new range of low-sugar sweets and chocolates is being planned by Cadbury Schweppes to meet the biddes of health-conscious consumers. It wants to raise spending on the "lite sweets" market by 66 per cent by 2009. Business, page 40

Cardinal rule

The Pope has begun taking soundings in England and Wales for a successor to the Archbishop of Westminster, Cardinal Cormac Murphy-O'Connor, who is expected to retire in 2009, *The Times* has learnt. News, page 9

Madeleine chaos

The investigation into the disappearance of Madeleine McCann was in chaos after the detective co-ordinating the hunt was charged with criminal offences over another notorious missing child case. News, page 5

'For a great Britain Day we should think of the Blitz, dig for victory and wear sensible shoes'
Caitlin Moran
times2

All mouth and no trousers: Jeremy Clarkson on the Volkswagen Eos convertible
timesonline.co.uk/driving

Unbelievable – my second Formula One victory in as many weeks, this time at the US Grand Prix.

Left Talking fun with Adrian Sutil, my good friend from Formula Three days.

Above Time for a laugh with my race engineer Phil Prew.

Above That champagne feeling – a fine moment.

Taking pole at Silverstone was a special moment.

Above Every second counts inside the McLaren garage.

Right Thanking my amazing fans at Silverstone.

Below right My dad's smile says it all.

Below My fans at the British Grand Prix were truly amazing.

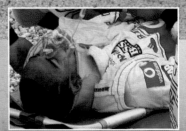

'Helpless – as my car careered into the tyre wall after a wheel failure at the Nürburgring. '

in those conditions, but it was seriously wet. Luckily, I managed
to keep the engine running and then, even more luckily, a crane
was able to set me free so I could rejoin the race, a lap down. A
big thank you to the Nürburgring marshals for that! Now that
the FIA have banned assistance from cranes, I guess I will go
down in history as the last Formula One driver to be hoisted
back into a race after flying off the track.

Then, after all that, the race was red-flagged. It was one of
those days filled with incidents. It was chaos really. There was
so much water on the circuit at some places that it was like trying to drive in a river. Cars just aquaplaned off the track and
there were a whole series of drivers who went off at turn one.
The conditions were claiming car after car, but some managed
to recover and rejoin. After the restart, I pushed as much as I
could to catch up, but when you are almost a lap down you
really have to rely on other drivers' misfortunes. I switched
from rain tyres back to dry tyres, hoping that the weather was
improving and the circuit was drying out, but it was too wet
and I skidded around and off and on everywhere. It was just a
battle with the elements really. In the end, after I passed a
Renault on the final lap, I finished the race in ninth.

It was the end of my podiums and I had not even scored a
point. It was difficult because I was driving what was, in
effect, a 'new' car, one that I had not tested myself and not got
used to driving. Everything on it was new after the big crash I
had in qualifying. But I went straight out in it and had to learn
my way around in the rain without actually knowing the car

was right. I just pushed as hard as I could right to the final lap. Instead of leading the championship by twelve points, as I had been before the race, I was now only two points ahead because Fernando won the race.

I did feel I had learned a lot in the conditions and after my big accident in qualifying. I remember reporters asking me how I felt at the end of it all and I managed to put on a smile and talk about the learning experience I had been through. I had arrived feeling a bit sick, then had a big crash, then a puncture, gone off into the gravel and then driven in the rain. I learned ten times as much in that one afternoon than I would have during a whole weekend in a normal race. I had told everybody in the paddock, right from day one, that my luck would not last forever and that sooner or later I would finish off the podium. It can't always be a perfect weekend, scoring points and podiums, race after race after race. One disappointing weekend like that was inevitable. I just hoped it was my one really bad race of the year and that after all those problems we would have a smooth and trouble-free weekend of sunshine in Hungary. Little did I know . . .

CHAPTER

STRIFE

'Ron asked me to allow Fernando to pass. But I was thinking "Where is he? I'm not slowing down if he can't keep up." I could sense that Ron was unhappy, but I was like, "Well, Fernando's miles behind, you know" and so I went for it.'

THE FIRST TIME I MET FERNANDO WAS IN 2006 while I was in GP2. I was having dinner with my dad at the Conrad Hotel Istanbul and he was on his way to his table, and while passing he came by and said, 'Hello, I'm Fernando.' He was the World Champion, he was fighting to win the title for a second time. I was pleased to meet him as he was a great driver and a great competitor. He was joining McLaren, and I had a lot of respect for his achievements. So I was pleased he stopped. It really surprised me that he had the time to come over to me and say hello. I was quite impressed with that.

Obviously, I really wanted the seat next to him in the McLaren team and equally I was very keen to prove myself to be worthy of it, if and when the time came. For me, that meant I had to show myself as a driver who could handle racing alongside Fernando and do well. But also I wanted to have a good relationship with him anyway; it is much better for everyone involved if there is a good level of trust and friendship between drivers in the team.

I did not see much more of Fernando until winter testing before the start of the 2007 season. He arrived in January. I was his new Formula One team-mate at McLaren and I think I was a bit quicker than him in testing, but he did not seem to be too fussed by that. It was an interesting time because I knew he would be quick – but I felt I was quick, too.

It was great for me to have the chance in my first year in Formula One to work alongside a champion like Fernando. And, of course, I learned a lot from him; we would share data from both of our cars in order to figure out the best setting for each of us. From the data it was possible to see where I was losing time and, therefore, where I could gain it. Being his team-mate and working alongside him was a great motivation, too. All of my former team-mates had been hugely competitive people and the challenge, and excitement, comes from having to find the answers to the most important question: 'Just how far do I need to push myself to beat that person and just how far can I go?'

I did not need a settling-in period, because I had been with McLaren and Mercedes-Benz for about ten years and already I felt I was part of the team. That was another advantage for me. I needed it, too, because in our sport the person you measure yourself against first, and have to beat first, is your own team-mate. As a rookie, I knew I needed to have some positives on my side to take on and beat a two-times World Champion. When you come up through the series of junior motorsport, particularly in GP2 and the Formula Three Euroseries, you get to see the world of Formula One close-up so you do not go into the job blind. I had spoken with two of my good friends Nico Rosberg and Robert Kubica about their experiences from 2006, when they raced in Formula One, so I knew what to expect in a lot of ways. That helped me, but it did not prepare me for Fernando and the way things worked out in Hungary.

That weekend at the Hungaroring is almost as unbelievable now as it seemed back then. I was the faster driver the whole weekend. I was faster than everyone, including Fernando. I was confident that I was definitely going to outqualify him. After the first two qualifying periods I was on provisional pole with time left for one last quick lap. I knew I had at least three-tenths in me when I came in.

At the start of final qualifying my engineer Phil Prew told me, 'If you get to the end of the pit lane first, you have to let Fernando past.' That was what the team wanted. So I got to the end of pit lane, knowing I had to let him past, and I thought: 'Where? Where shall I let Fernando past?' I accelerated, got round the first corner, and thought where is he? Then he appeared and I could see Kimi was right up his tail and, as I'd been overtaken by the Ferraris a couple of times this year at the beginning of qualifying, I thought, 'I don't want to lose my place because that could really ruin my opportunity for pole.'

Ron asked me to allow Fernando to pass. But I was thinking 'Where is he? I'm not slowing down if he can't keep up.' I could sense that Ron was unhappy, but I was like, 'Well, Fernando's miles behind, you know' and so I went for it.

On the final pit stop in qualifying period three, I came into the pits and I thought Fernando was doing something strange but I did not know what was going on. I could see him looking in his mirrors. He was still stationary in the pit box having been given the all-clear to go, so I knew something was wrong but it all happened so quickly that I had not given it a thought until I was heading out for my final run. I remember I had to stop behind Fernando in the pit box and put it into neutral while waiting for him. Eventually, he left the pit box and I got my new tyres on and went out, but midway through my lap my radio engineer told me I would not make it to the flag in time to start my final run for pole. It was too late. Fernando had just posted the fastest qualifying time. I had come across the line just a few seconds too late to complete a lap and beat Fernando to pole position. Shoot! I came on the radio saying, 'Very, very funny, guys!' I could not believe it. I just thought that Ron had got me back for ignoring his instructions, but it was not

like that. Instead, it was Fernando getting me back for not
letting him pass earlier.

During the Hungarian Grand Prix weekend I had to keep
my mind in gear for the race. I did not want to fill myself with
negative energy. So even when I was asked about the grid positions, and what had happened, I kept a smile on my face as
much as I could. I knew that the outside was the dirty side,
and it was going to give a possible advantage to the guys on
the inside. But I just concentrated on thinking positive –
laying down rubber on that side of the track, cleaning it up,
doing the best I could. That was before the FIA, or the race
officials, decided to intervene.

I think some of the press guys were sniffing a bit of a
story anyway. There were quite a few interesting questions at
the press conference after the session. People were also talking
a lot about the Ferrari controversy and I told them there was
nothing I could say. I knew nothing about it, not then anyway.
Even though there was so much stuff happening that weekend, below the surface, it did not reach me. I just concentrated
on my job.

After all the media conferences, I went to my normal
engineers' meeting and you can imagine the feelings that
were aroused! There was a lot of stuff still unfolding then. It
was a really difficult situation. There were a few discussions,
to put it mildly. The team explained it all to me from their
point of view and I apologized for the decision I took when
I was out there on my own. I apologized to Ron and said it

would not happen again. But even then, as we talked it all over, there were a lot of other things going on that were going to cause as big a storm in the team all over again the next day.

One of these was the story, printed in some of the Sunday newspapers, which said there had been a row between Ron and me over the team radio, a row littered with bad language and swear words. I do not know where these kinds of stories started from because it was not true at all. Someone had claimed that they had seen a transcript of the radio communication during qualifying when the team had not even produced one. It caused a lot of heartache, adding to the problems that were already piling up.

After qualifying, the Stewards took the decision to investigate what had happened during qualifying. Both Fernando and I were called to see the Clerk of the Course to explain. Ron was called up also. The meetings went on for what seemed like forever and eventually we were allowed to leave and so I returned to my hotel. I was at the hotel late that evening, on the Saturday, when I heard what had happened. The Stewards found that Fernando had unnecessarily impeded me during the pit stop. It was for that he received his penalty. They had moved Fernando back five places on the grid and disqualified the team from scoring Constructors' Championship points. For me, it was like my worst nightmare.

I tried to keep things as normal as possible the next morning. I went to all of them in the garage and everyone, but two people, shook my hand and said, 'Let's go for it.' Then I said 'Let's do it.' It was strange, almost a bit funny strange; and not an ideal way of going into a race. After all, all I did was what I thought best at the time in trying to protect my own position.

I started from pole and I knew I had to concentrate and just do my job. I think it worked out reasonably well in the end, but it was not the kind of victory that put a smile on everyone's face. Too much had gone on before the race. I managed to lead from the start and defend when I had to and control the race from the front. It was such an eventful rollercoaster of a weekend, with so much political stuff going on, that it was really emotional for us all in the team. I had a good start, we had great pace, as I expected, and in the first stint we pulled clear and made a gap so I could control the race. That left me able to look after my tyres and the fuel. I had a steering problem in the second stint, but it was okay and I managed to stay in front of Kimi to the end. Kimi pushed me really hard throughout the race and hounded me all the way. The Ferraris had a good amount of pace and it was tough to stay ahead all the time but I led every lap and stayed in front.

Afterwards, obviously, there were a lot of people asking me again about the controversy in qualifying and how I felt about it. I just told the truth. I said I was worried by everything and I came into the race feeling a bit like there was a big cloud over my mind. It was more difficult than usual to stay focused because I knew the team were not winning any points. I also got asked about Fernando and said how much I had always admired him for his achievements. But I also said that it seemed he had not been speaking to me since Saturday so I did not know if he had a problem. He had finished fourth so obviously he was not too happy anyway. Neither was Ron. We had discussed all of the events of Saturday pretty much soon after it all happened, but he had also been involved in a lot of other stuff that morning, before the race, that I only heard about later on. He had listened to me and he said he respected my point of view. We started with a clean slate on the Sunday and I am sure my win helped a bit – even if it did not show that much all around the team. There was so much pressure by then and we still delivered.

I think that weekend sorted a few things out in a strange way. When you have the two most competitive people in the team, possibly the two most competitive people around, both wanting to win, it puts the team under immense pressure and in the mind sometimes it can appear that one driver is favoured over the other. That is why sometimes I felt Fernando was favoured and I am sure he felt the same with me. I did not want to fall out with Fernando and I hoped we could speak and carry on as well as possible as team-mates. I think I am easy to get along with, I do not hold grudges about anyone but I felt that if he did not want to speak to me or to have a decent working relationship, then that was up to him.

After Hungary, I called Fernando before we went off on holiday, and said, 'Do we need to meet up?' I thought I would take the initiative. 'Look, I don't have a problem with you but let's sort this out.' He did call me back, saying he agreed that we should meet up, but he was busy that week in Spain. So it had to be the week of the next race in Turkey. At least that meant, or so I thought, that I could have a holiday without any more hassle and grief from the politics of that race in Budapest. Some hope! As I had to learn quickly, even when on holiday, a Formula One driver, especially the guy who is leading the championship, is a target for the paparazzi.

After the holidays we did meet up. We were in Turkey again and staying in the Conrad, that same hotel where we first met in 2006. We went up to his room because he did not want to meet at the bar. I said, 'Look, I don't have any issues with you. I have got total respect for you. I want to beat you, but that doesn't stand in the way of the respect that I have for you.' He said much the same, we shook hands and that was it, all sorted, and so we went to the track and told everyone how it was. It was a much better weekend from that point of view, but nothing was really very different below the surface.

Ron was always pushing me to help Fernando feel happy and welcome because Ron wanted Fernando to feel good in the team, which is what we all wanted very much. So I did try, I tried a lot, but I was not really getting anywhere with him. In the end, I just told Ron, 'I tried to speak to him, but I am not going to go out of my way and de-focus myself to make him happy. I'm going to focus on my dream . . .'

It should not have been like that – for either of us – but it was the way things went and Hungary was the real lowest point. When we arrived in Budapest that weekend, everything was just as normal as it had been the last couple of races. You know, very professional: 'Hi Lewis,' 'Hi Fernando,' and that was it. You would never have imagined what was going to happen on that weekend. It was just so extraordinary.

I heard a while afterwards that Ron and Fernando had had a row – during which Fernando stated that he had emails in his possession that he claimed would incriminate the team. Like everyone else I was just amazed. It was really extraordinary that it happened on the morning of the race, as well.

We went to Turkey, then Monza and then to Spa-Francorchamps. The whole Ferrari controversy thing erupted in Italy, where Fernando's involvement in some of the events was made clear and the existence of certain emails became known (although I had not seen them), and then he did not go to Paris for the hearing despite having been requested to by the team. At Spa he showed me another side to his character in the race. At the start of the race, coming out of the first corner, Fernando ran me wide and off the circuit.

From then on, it was clear that anything could happen. If he wanted to be as aggressive as that, then so could I. It was not healthy, but I felt I could be strong and aggressive without taking any unnecessary risks. It was a real pity that things had come to this. I was finding it all a bit hard to understand.

CHAPTER **14**

FAME

'Despite what has been said in the newspapers, moving abroad is not about tax. I love England and I am happy to pay my tax if I live there. Obviously there are places that are better for tax reasons: places where a lot of Formula One drivers live like Monaco, Dubai or Switzerland. But money is not the decider in my life – quality of life is. I would happily move anywhere in the world to regain some quality of life.'

IT HAS BEEN AN INCREDIBLE JOURNEY from winning the GP2 Championship in 2006 to leading the Formula One World Championship in just one year.

I feel that I am still the same person I was a year ago but clearly on the outside my life is perceived as completely different. I cannot believe the people I have met this year, charitable people, friendly people, fans and new friends. I have also met some incredibly famous people and am still struggling to believe it.

The three-week break before the Turkish Grand Prix is a chance for everyone in Formula One to take a holiday. After all the travelling, the testing and the racing we all get a chance for a bit of a rest and some down time. For some of the drivers, it is just a good opportunity to stay at home and recharge the batteries, but for me, after all that had gone on in Hungary, I felt like I needed to get away.

The original idea was for me to go with my family to their holiday home in Portugal. I also considered going away with my friends for a lads' holiday, but when I reconsidered, I thought it was a bad idea at the mid-part of the season. So, having been lucky enough to be invited as a guest of the Ojjeh family on their family boat in the Mediterranean, I chose instead to go to sea and escape from everything for a while.

I arrived on holiday with Mansour's family thinking I was going to be 100 per cent relaxed: I would be at sea, away from the outside world and enjoying myself. And I did – but it was not even a day before the paparazzi appeared and that was it. My hopes of a quiet time to relax and just have some fun and be a normal 22-year-old were over before they had started. It was a kind of shock to the system.

Everyone else was having fun outdoors, doing all sorts of watersports, and I was pretty much forced to stay inside all day to protect the people that I was with and to make sure that their holiday was not ruined by my presence. Every day the paparazzi surrounded the boat and would chase us everywhere. We were moving around the Mediterranean visiting many places and they followed us all the time. And in every port, as soon as we pulled in, there was a camera waiting. There always seemed to be five boats or more whizzing around us. Maybe I was naïve. I had never experienced anything like it before and I did not really know what to do and was not prepared.

It was disappointing to hear that pictures of me with Mansour's daughter Sarah were published in the press. After all, the Ojjehs were on holiday and they kindly invited me along but I am sure they were not expecting the press intrusion that accompanied me. I could not go and sunbathe, or stand next to any of the girls, without having my picture taken. The pictures were bad enough but the stories that were printed with them were just unfair, untrue and hurtful to everyone involved.

Pictures of me and Sarah Ojjeh just messing around in the sea were made to look like something completely different. I was having some innocent fun and a good time and the papers tried to make it seem as if all sorts of things were going on. In actual fact, there were three Ojjeh daughters on the boat and they all had their boyfriends with them. And what nobody could see from the pictures was that there were more than a dozen people on the boat, all playing around and throwing each other in the sea and that kind of thing, including Mansour. And they say the camera never lies . . .

I was really concerned that I was ruining the Ojjehs' family holiday but Mansour was so cool about it and so relaxed. He just said, 'Don't worry about it, buddie.' But I did worry! I thought the Ojjehs would probably want me to go, but I knew they would never ask me to, so I suggested to them that it might be best if I went home. I was on the verge of leaving, but the whole family begged me to stay. I felt torn, but they wanted me to stay. It was a really strange experience, but I had to learn how to deal with it. Eventually, I did manage to forget I was being watched and I think, as the days went by, the attention did die down a bit. But I had never felt so miserable in those circumstances when I was supposed to be relaxing and enjoying myself.

I ate well, trained a bit, tried to relax and just looked after myself. The girls were amazed at first that I liked to eat every two hours or so, but that was because of the amount of exercise I was doing. I was just keeping myself in good shape. They also discovered I have a really sweet tooth and I got a bit of a teasing. I also like hot and spicy food, so that was another talking-point and we had a lot of laughs when Mansour and I had a contest, eating very hot food and sauces. I am not going to say who won! I will just say we are both very competitive people and we had a big laugh. Everyone did.

I love swimming and it was just so cool to be there, in the Mediterranean, in the summer, and just to be able to swim in the sea. I do not like to stay in the water too long although I am a confident swimmer. There is always something in the back of my mind that keeps me alert in water. I can do all the jumping off the boat and all that stuff, no problem, but I do keep my senses alert to any possible dangers – maybe I've watched too many horror movies or something . . .

After the holiday I returned to England to find that the whole of my holiday week had been covered in nearly every major daily paper, not only in the UK but all over Europe and the US. There were loads of pictures of me in the papers implying that I was sleeping with this woman, or that woman. None of the stories were true – if only! The week after I returned to England, I went to the cinema with some friends I had not seen for a few weeks. As I was leaving the cinema the snappers were waiting outside. I warned my friends and tried to walk separately from them to protect them but one picture was taken with my friend's girlfriend in the background and the papers made out that I was dating a mystery woman and that the other guy was my bodyguard. In fact, I was out with my friend Mohammed and his fiancée. I do not have a bodyguard. So, according to the paparazzi, not only was I dating one of the Ojjeh girls, who happened to have a boyfriend, but I was out with my best friend's fiancée too! I wouldn't mind so much if the stories were true or I had actually done something for people to write about, but it all just got ridiculous. I was doing normal things that were not worth reporting but that clearly was not 'news' so it was all spiced up – but it was not fair on the people involved. Not only was my privacy invaded but the private lives of my friends were also invaded and they didn't ask for that or expect it.

I have not bought any fancy cars and I have not dated any fancy women and I do not have a home in Monaco. I still live alone, have a group of very loyal and close friends, have a fantastic dream job and try to lead as ordinary a life as possible.

Stuff that is not even close to the truth is frustrating and damaging. You know everyone will read it, that people you care about will read it, but you cannot do anything about it. I particularly felt for my ex-girlfriend Jo who was hounded with all these untrue stories about me and other women, and about me and her. Imagine how she must have been feeling and what she must have been going through. It was not a nice time for either of us. We are still great friends and we talk when we can, but the papers made out that I was cheating on her and that was just not right. It had a devastating effect on us both as we were extremely close and loyal to each other throughout our time together. I am extremely sorry for Jo, she does not deserve what has been printed in the press but now we know, and now I hope everyone who reads this book will also know the truth.

In any case, I have great faith in the public making up their own minds. I believe that the public know the real truth about me and that is what they see about me and my family and my racing.

I now also have people following me in my car. A couple of times I have had to burn rubber and leave them behind and that's not good because it can be dangerous. In that situation, you just do not know what is going on. You almost have to fear for your life a little bit and I do not want to live my life like that. I would rather completely avoid it in the best possible way and have a place where I can feel safe from intrusion. So I did some research to find out what other people do in similar situations.

It was then that I first started thinking seriously about leaving England, leaving the UK, to live abroad. A lot of people had told me it was the best thing to do as most Formula One drivers move abroad anyway. I would not be in the papers all the time if I were not there to be photographed. It was quite exciting in a way, the idea of living abroad. It made me feel quite free just to think about it. I knew I could go anywhere I wanted and, heeding a lot of good advice, I finally reached my decision: I would move to Switzerland.

Despite what has been said in the newspapers, moving abroad is not about tax. I love England and I am happy to pay my tax if I live there. Obviously there are places that are better for tax reasons: places where a lot of Formula One drivers live like Monaco, Dubai or Switzerland. But money is not the decider in my life – quality of life is. I would happily move anywhere in the world to regain some quality of life.

Switzerland has a great feel. I had never been there until this year and I absolutely loved it. I thought it was such a cool, chilled-out place. I imagined my life there and it was all sweet things. I just thought about what I would do in the winter, the testing, the training, swimming in lakes, the mountains to climb . . . It is beautiful. The quality of life is really good. Ever since I went on holiday to Austria I have always liked that sort of place: nice in the winter, nice in the summer, just nice all round. In Switzerland, you get a bit of snow, a bit of sun. Anyone who has been there knows how wonderful it is and also how relaxed. It just felt good to me.

Even in the couple of days I spent there, when I went to check it out, all the people were so welcoming. I thought I would not be noticed in Switzerland, but I had quite a few people approach me in the street. It was pleasant though and I did not mind that. I thought it was a wicked place and I could live there. So, I made arrangements for Swiss residency and moved to Switzerland.

I am away working most of the year – at races, testing, doing promotional events and travelling. I would only spend about eighty days in England and so it made sense to move abroad. The days I do spend in England, I am generally just chilling with my family and friends.

Moving away from England and my family and friends and everything I knew and loved was not an easy decision. In the end, when I weighed it up, I realized it was the best thing to do for now. I am British so I can always come back! I love my fans, my fantastic British fans, and that will never change, but I needed to move for my own good.

So I had all these thoughts – the hassle from the paparazzi, my move to Switzerland and so on – buzzing in my head during that summer holiday period and in the lead up to my next race in Istanbul, Turkey.

I really like Istanbul. I had a great GP2 race there in 2006 when, after spinning early on, I worked my way up from last to second. Having that experience under my belt eased my mind so I felt good immediately and I was pretty quick in practice.

Qualifying was pretty close and tightly contested and as we edged towards the closing minutes I harboured a thought that I might have done enough with a lap of 1 minute 27.373 seconds. But Felipe went out and made best use of the Ferrari's speed on that track and took pole with a lap of 1:27.329. The gap was just 0.044 seconds – that close.

One of the things the team did differently in qualifying was to introduce the use of separate pit boxes and crews so that there could not be a repeat of what had happened in Hungary. It was just one of the things we decided to do and I thought it worked pretty well.

Although I did not take pole, I felt reasonably satisfied with the lap I did. I pushed all the way, but felt I lost some time in the last corner, which can be pretty tricky. Still, the outcome was good for me and for the team. Fernando was fourth on the grid.

The team had worked hard on the car over the summer break so I was happy to get them on the front row and, of course, I was happy to be ahead of Fernando. In the race we had the pace of the Ferraris but they still managed to get a one two. My start was not good. Kimi squeezed past me and I was stuck in third. I could keep up, but I lost a bit of speed being behind him all the time and I could never overtake him. Still, I was heading for a comfortable podium, or at least I thought I was, until I saw bits of rubber flying off my front right tyre.

I had noticed something was flapping on the tyre on the exit of turn eight – it was a big surprise to me as I did not feel anything happening. Then as I was braking into turn nine the tyre just exploded as soon as I hit the brakes. There was nothing I could do. The wheel just locked up and I was very lucky I did not end up in the gravel or, even worse, in a wall. Fortunately the run-off area was tarmacked and so I had time to save myself and my car from harm. I locked up all the wheels to get the car stopped and then I just tried to nurse it back to the pits. The tyre was flapping around everywhere, getting worse and worse all the time. There was also quite a big chunk missing from the front wing.

I was pretty lucky because most people, when they lose a tyre, also break their front wing or their suspension. That was on my mind when I was going slowly back to the pits. I knew I had to be very careful, but at the same time I wanted to get in as soon as possible without losing too many places. I could not really steer, though, and Fernando and Nick Heidfeld both passed me. Finally, I fought the car back to the pits after almost hitting the wall and we got the tyre off. The team decided not to change the broken wing because we could not afford to lose any more time. It was the right decision, but the wing gave me trouble for the rest of the race. I had huge understeer so I could not catch Nick Heidfeld and, in the end, I finished fifth. Felipe won from Kimi and Fernando was third. At first I was disappointed, but considering my tyre had blown up in the race and I had nearly lost everything, I realized fifth was not too bad.

It was my second expensive and dramatic incident of the season, after the Nürburgring episode, but I felt it was not a problem. Fernando, I could see, was pretty pleased to leave Turkey five points behind me because he knew he was very lucky to finish third, but apart from that it was a fairly positive weekend. I had done a good job in qualifying and then made the best of some bad luck in the race.

August had been a tough month. I had faced some hard decisions and dealt with some issues. And I had made perhaps my most difficult decision of all – to leave England.

CHAPTER

CONTROVERSY

'I never thought I would ever say that I had found
something I disliked about Formula One, but I found
the controversy difficult to handle.'

I WANTED TO DO MORE TALKING ON THE TRACK than ever before. With all the politics surrounding the team and the distractions this caused, I wanted to tell everyone that it was important for us to do our business on the track, which is where it matters.

When we got to Monza for the Italian Grand Prix, Ferrari's home race, the spotlight was really on us. Monza was, as expected, packed with loyal Italian fans, though I was surprised to find there were quite a few Italian McLaren supporters and Lewis Hamilton supporters there. Inevitably, the main talking point among the media was the controversy with Ferrari.

When the rumours started and the story broke back in July just before Silverstone, it was all very vague. It was along the lines that there was going to be an investigation in a matter involving Ferrari and McLaren. It didn't seem to be a big deal. I certainly didn't know what was going on at the time as I just kept my head down and got on with my job. It was such a busy week for me that I did not have time to think about it. Things are often investigated and that's the end of the matter. There was nothing to lead me to believe that this would be any different.

Then the week after Silverstone, the FIA announced that my team was charged with having unauthorized possession of documents and confidential information belonging to Ferrari. This came as something of a shock to me and I was obviously concerned. There were a number of rumours as to what this might involve. I didn't know the details of the allegation but, from my knowledge of McLaren, I found such a notion incredible. Whenever I was asked about any of this, I would express my full support for the team. I had been with McLaren, Mercedes-Benz and Ron Dennis for nearly ten years so I knew these guys well. Dishonesty is just not part of the McLaren and Mercedes-Benz way of life in my opinion.

The week after the Nürburgring the team went to Paris for the FIA hearing. It was something that had concerned me in the sense that my team were in trouble, but I just did not see what all the fuss was about. For those of you, like me, who are in the dark about this, this is my understanding from what I have read in the press.

Apparently this whole business related to some sort of dossier belonging to Ferrari which had been received by an employee at McLaren, from an employee at Ferrari. At that first FIA hearing, nothing was proved and therefore my team were not punished. It was judged that the McLaren employee was in possession of Ferrari data at his home, but the FIA said that it could not be proved that it was used at all or that McLaren gained any advantage from it. The official verdict said: 'There is insufficient evidence that this information was used in such a way as to interfere improperly with the FIA Formula One World Championship. We therefore impose no penalty.' For a few days, it seemed like that was the end of it, but then I heard that an appeal was on its way.

Everybody at McLaren and Mercedes-Benz has worked so hard this and last year to develop the best car on the grid. I rarely get involved in the in-depth technical stuff surrounding the car development even though I am interested in everything to do with the car.

The whole Ferrari controversy thing had gone on during the Turkish Grand Prix, but it was still in the background. Then after the race I received a formal letter from the FIA in connection with the ongoing investigation. The letter stated:

The FIA have subsequently been made aware of an allegation that one or more McLaren drivers may be in possession, or that such drivers have recently been in possession, of written evidence relevant to this investigation.

For me this took things onto a different level. I couldn't believe that I had actually received this letter from the FIA. I thought, 'I don't know anything, what's this all about?' The letter demanded a formal response and warned that if it came to light that I had withheld any potentially relevant information, serious consequences could follow. Well, just imagine how that felt, me in my first year of Formula One and I'm already getting potential career-threatening letters . . .

I had to explain how information was communicated between the team and myself; what, if any, Ferrari information I may have had at any stage; and to go through all my emails and correspondence just in case I had inadvertently received something that might be relevant, even though I did not realize it at the time. I considered the matter carefully with my dad and my lawyers and provided my response to FIA President Max Mosley. I then got on with my sponsor duties and was looking forward to Monza and thought no more about it because there was nothing as far as I was concerned to worry about. You know when you are innocent – that's how I felt, confident that we were innocent.

Just after I had sent in my letter to the FIA, they announced that the World Motor Sport Council would reconvene for a Paris hearing in just under two weeks' time, which was the Thursday of the Spa race weekend. That was the date when the original Ferrari appeal had been due to be heard.

We were in the beginning of the Italian Grand Prix week, and so that really got the media, and especially the Italian media, excited. It meant the week leading up to the race in Monza was tense. All of my focus was directed at doing the best job I could. Naturally, as a Vodafone McLaren Mercedes driver, I wanted to beat the Ferraris on their home ground. It was nothing personal, just business. It was the same I'm sure for Ferrari when they were at Silverstone. I remember thinking how much of a boost it would be to my team if we were to beat Ferrari that weekend.

I was concerned by all the speculation. If you just sat down and thought about it, it was quite possible that I could have everything I had worked for and everything the team had worked for taken away. I never thought I would ever say that I had found something I disliked about Formula One, but I found the controversy difficult to handle.

To me, it all seemed so unfair. But I was proud of the way we refused to react to all the stuff that we were forced to take that weekend. There were all kinds of stunts going on, like having Italian court officers and police guards arriving in the paddock just before qualifying with papers to deliver to the team, but we stayed strong and we did our talking on the track. It was, 'Lewis, what about this? Lewis, what about that?' I could understand that most of them supported Ferrari and so, for them, the biggest story was about the spying allegations, but it was a terrible atmosphere and there were a lot of wild rumours circulating. I was just not interested.

As usual, I just concentrated on my job. My goal was to beat the Ferraris out there on the track and I felt really motivated. I was part of the team and I hated being called a cheat and it is the same for McLaren. It is the worst thing anyone can be accused of. I never, ever cheat and I hated it. But I could not react. It is the way I have always dealt with things. My dad always told me to do my talking on the track and that is exactly what I did.

I knew I had a chance to beat the Ferraris and finish in front of Fernando, but it was not quite a perfect race weekend for me. I was on the lighter fuel load in qualifying, but I did not get the job done on my final qualifying lap and I ended up second on the grid behind Fernando. Then, I got a bad start in the race and saw Felipe's Ferrari shoot past me into second. I knew I had to act fast and I managed to outbrake Felipe and Fernando into the first chicane. I was past Felipe and had a good chance to get Fernando, but Felipe clipped me and sent me over the second part of the chicane. I lost that opportunity and nearly got taken out of the race!

The Safety Car came out for an early incident and I had a second opportunity at the restart to improve my position but Fernando made sure he pulled out enough of a gap at the last corner to stay clear. I never had another chance to have a proper go at Fernando and it was quite frustrating. In the middle stint of the race, I started having a problem with my tyres, which I had flat-spotted. Everything was vibrating. We really did not want another Turkey situation so I pitted early, played it safe and made sure to bag some points. That allowed Kimi to get in front of me, but I put in some hard laps after getting out of the pits and created a chance for myself.

I knew I only had one shot, and I managed to take it – I late-braked Kimi at the end of the straight and took my second place back. That is where I finished in the end, which was respectable. A one-two for the team at Monza was a great way for us to hit back at all the stuff going on off the track. We had proved our strength in qualifying and to do it again in the race had put the icing on the cake.

I flew home from Monza that Sunday night and it was only afterwards that the full implications of the hearing sank in. In the worst-case scenario, according to what we were reading and what we were being told, McLaren could have been thrown out of Formula One for a couple of years and I could have been out of a job. I had just arrived in Formula One! Everything was going so well for me and now I faced complete disaster. The year had been so amazing. I was in my rookie season, I was challenging for the championship, and it could all easily have crumbled around me. The whole team had worked so hard all season and it might all have been for nothing.

The politics of Formula One can be too difficult at times. It is the only thing I really dislike about the sport. At Monza, it was crazy. Ron, who had always been very, very loyal to me, who had given me all my opportunities and been so great for me, was under attack. His team was being threatened over something he insisted they had not done. I have never had any reasons to doubt him, and I found this all very stressful and upsetting.

To be honest, from everything that was coming out in the press and through rumour and gossip, it didn't look good for the team. I was very worried. The next week I was asked if I would provide a witness statement for the team. It then turned out we were all being asked to give evidence. Yet more lawyers became involved. I was becoming concerned for my position and decided that I should be represented at the Paris hearing, just in case the decision went against the team. I wanted to have my say about any punishment, particularly if it was going to affect me. At the same time, I was having to get on with preparing for Spa and carrying out my sponsor duties as well as numerous other things. This was really disruptive for me.

The tension was building up and it was quite difficult to juggle all that I had on. The hearing was fixed for Paris on the Thursday, but I was having to deal with matters until after midnight on Tuesday. On the Wednesday morning first thing, I flew over to my home in Switzerland to deal with some issues and then had to fly back to Paris to meet my lawyers on the Wednesday evening. Even while I was in Switzerland I kept having to be interrupted to deal with matters and take decisions.

The evening before the hearing I stayed in the same hotel as the team. All the senior management of the team were there, together with several engineers, who were going to have to give evidence, and the company's shareholders. Pedro de la

Rosa was also there. It was only then that I found out that Fernando would not be attending the hearing, although I was told that he had given a written statement. I was told that he had been asked to attend (as we all had) but he said he had other arrangements.

At the hotel, I sat and talked with many of the McLaren engineers and Pedro. We avoided the subject of the hearing the following day, but everybody was very tense and nervous. I didn't see much of Ron or Martin as they were involved in other meetings with their lawyers. I then had to meet with my lawyers to go through matters relating to the hearing. What was strange is that I knew that there were issues relating to some emails and other things, but as they contained confidential information, I was not even allowed to see them before I gave evidence!

By the time I went to bed I was exhausted, but then I had to get up early the following day for another meeting and then travel to the WMSC Hearing at the FIA Headquarters

When the car pulled up I saw the huge pack of photographers and just trying to get through the crowd was a mission. When we arrived at the FIA Headquarters there were masses of boxes of paper. I had to go to the waiting area to sign in with security. Going down the corridors of the FIA Headquarters I saw lots of framed pictures and photographs. I was fascinated, looking through the history of racing as I walked along. One photo in particular caught my eye: it was a scene from probably the early to mid 1950s and it was of a Maserati racing round the streets of Monaco and there were no safety barriers. The car was almost touching the side of the buildings as it raced past. It was spectacular and so unlike the Monaco streets today in a Formula One race meeting.

The waiting room was packed with people all looking very serious and worried. The WMSC called everyone in but as I was a witness I had to sit outside with all the other people from my team who were giving evidence. The Ferrari witnesses were in another room and so I didn't see them.

After a while everybody came back out saying that the start had been put back because many of the members of the WMSC had not been able to read the McLaren evidence which some had not received until nearly midnight the day before.

After about half an hour everybody went back in the room and I stayed outside with the other witnesses. It was a nerve-wracking time for everyone as we waited outside, eagerly trying to anticipate when we would be called in to do our bit and get it over and done with.

When you are sitting waiting for something, time drags so slowly. We were curious to know what was happening in the large meeting room next door.

The doors opened and everybody flooded out. We were told that witnesses would start to give evidence next and my lawyers asked if I could go first because I was anxious to get to Spa and it was now already early afternoon.

The hearing reconvened and I went in expecting to be grilled. Ian Mill QC was representing McLaren and Nigel Tozzi

QC was representing Ferrari. The huge ordeal of my having to give evidence on this occasion went like this:

Ian Mill QC: Mr Hamilton, you have a copy of your statement in front of you. Please look at the second page. Is that your signature toward the bottom of this page?

Me: It is.

Ian Mill: Have you read this statement?

Me: I have.

Ian Mill: Are the contents true to the best of your knowledge and belief?

Me: Yes.

Ian Mill: Thank you.

Max Mosley: Mr Tozzi, do you wish to ask any questions of Mr Hamilton?

Nigel Tozzi QC: I have no questions for Mr Hamilton.

Max Mosley: Does anyone have any questions for Mr Hamilton? Thank you, Mr Hamilton.

All the worries and concerns I had had in the preparation for the hearing and it was all over and done for me in a flash. I was surprised that Ferrari didn't even ask me any questions.

That was it, I was free to go and so I headed off for Spa and left instructions with my legal team about the representations to make in the event that things did not go well for McLaren. I waited to hear the news.

I arrived at Spa-Francorchamps and went through near-enough the same preparation as I could for the Belgian Grand Prix. Fernando was already at the circuit – I had obviously left a number of other members of the team in Paris. It was very intense because everyone was wondering what the decision was going to be from Paris – and waiting for that seemed to go on forever. I was walking round the Spa circuit that Thursday afternoon and called Pedro to see if there was any news. I was really unaware of what exactly was going on and wanted to know. He said, 'Oh, Lewis, it's not good for us, man. They said they were going to be throwing us all out – the team and the drivers.'

I was stunned. As I stood there, on that magnificent circuit through the sweeping forests in the Belgian Ardennes, I just could not take it in. I really feared the worst and felt that my first season could be wrecked. I was leading the championship and I was in a great position. It could all be ruined in an instant.

We all had a huge scare when wrong information about the decision had been published on the internet saying that McLaren and its drivers had been excluded from the championship.

The official announcement did not come until much later. And when it did, I realized my first feelings had been caused by a false alarm. Having said that, the punishment was very severe – the team were given a huge fine and thrown out of the 2007 Constructors' Championship. But we were allowed to keep our points in the Drivers' Championship. It meant that Fernando and I were still able to race and fight for the title.

It was terrible for the team, but Ron Dennis wanted to put it behind us as soon as possible. He talked about closure and said the interests of the sport were paramount and made it clear we were unlikely to appeal.

In a way, I was glad that it was over. The whole thing had been very stressful. I was just relieved that I had nothing to do with it. I was not involved in any of the emails or other stuff. Afterwards, I just tried to put it all out of my mind.

This was my first season in Formula One and all I wanted to do was to get on and race and for my team to be allowed to do the same. I believed in my team then, and still do now. McLaren are an honest team. Why were we given the biggest fine in motorsport history? I'll never really know or understand and neither will a lot of people but that's the way it ended.

The Belgian Grand Prix at Spa-Francorchamps is one of the great races on the Formula One calendar and it was the one I had looked forward to most of all. I got in the car and tried to do the best job I could. I loved the fact that I still had the opportunity to drive it and there was nothing that would stop me from driving it. There were no more threats. I knew I had won the races fair and square, and that the team had done a good job putting the car together. I knew we deserved the successes we had had because we had earned it the hard way.

Unfortunately, Belgium was not a good race for me. I set the car up all wrong and, to be honest, it was a bit of a disaster. The set-up was so bad I was struggling to drive the car and I knew it was totally my fault. There had been a test day at Spa a few weeks earlier and I had been quickest by far. Even the Ferraris could not keep up with my consistency that day. So when we went back to Belgium for the race, I stayed with that set-up and Fernando went down a different route – pretty much the one we had both been following all year.

It was my fault. My engineer can only do his job if I give him the correct information. He can only set the car up the way I want it and that is the way it works between us. I request the set-up and he has enough confidence in me to know that when I say 'I need x' then 'x' is what we have to do. If I say 'We need to go softer here, we need to change the springs' or whatever, he has the confidence in me to go ahead and do that. That weekend, I made a bad call and I paid for it. The car was still driveable, but it was very, very tricky to handle, especially on heavy fuel loads.

I could have used the distraction of the controversy with Ferrari as an excuse for setting the car up wrong, but I would not do that. It was a decision I had made back at the test and the court case did not affect it. Of course, having such a busy and stressful week running up to the race was not the best preparation, but I still prepared well enough. I did not have a single day off between the two races. I felt like I was fighting the car throughout practice and things were still pretty crap in qualifying. I was Q4 and Fernando was Q3. Even though Fernando was not that much quicker than me, he was a lot more consistent and it was a lot easier for him to look after his tyres and everything. He had an advantage and I knew that I had to do something a bit special to make up for that if I could. I needed to make a good start.

When the race started, I actually got a great start and I was right behind Felipe, who was second as we drove into La Source, the hairpin. I had pulled myself up alongside Fernando as we went round the corner. After everything else that had happened, I didn't believe he could still do anything that could surprise me – but he did! As we exited La Source, Fernando swung his car out across mine and effectively forced me off the track. He left me no room whatsoever. I can accept hard racing. You do not expect anybody to give you a position in Formula One, but I felt Fernando's move was unfair. There was plenty of room for us both and he pushed me as wide as he could. Fernando has himself complained about people making unfair moves and I thought here he is not practising what he preaches.

He complained, for example, about a move Felipe made at the Nürburgring this year. And there he is shoving me off the track! I took it in my stride and got on with the race. Luckily, I went off the track into a run-off area, so I could come back on without any damage, and I did not even lose much time. I considered having another go at him at the famous Eau Rouge corner as we accelerated away down the hill away from La Source. If I had lost my head, I would have done it, but it would have been stupid. It is impossible for two Formula One cars to go through there at once and it would have taken us both out. As we approached the corner, side by side, and driving flat out, I tucked in behind. Then I tried my best to get by him down the straight, but my chance had passed.

I think I was half-expecting Fernando to make a move, but it was still a surprise when it happened. Luckily, for me, I find it quite easy to handle my emotions when something like that happens. And when it does, you have to have a Plan B. Unfortunately, on that day at Spa with Fernando, the opportunity never came around again and I finished fourth. The Ferraris were incredibly quick and won the race.

Although it was still an okay weekend, it meant it was three in a row that Fernando had beaten me, at a time when I wanted to beat him more than ever. I was frustrated because of that and because I had not won since Hungary. I also wanted to sort out a few things to do with my own performance. I felt the championship was there for the taking, but I had to take each race as it came. I had to be composed but competitive.

So, the next day, I went straight into the factory to analyse, study and work on the data from the race weekend. Somewhere, something was going wrong. I worked with my race engineers for a few hours that day. We looked at the traction control settings, the differential settings, the whole set-up, the use of tyres, where I was braking, where I was losing time: everything we could think of that mattered. We just did the works. And it was worth it for me because I learned a lot about where we could improve and where I was going wrong. It made so much sense to me that I knew exactly what to do to put things right. I felt I had restored something and was ready for the challenge that lay ahead in Japan and China.

CHAPTER 16

PRESSURE

'Driving behind the Safety Car in those conditions in a Formula One race was new to me. Like everyone else in that race, I was under a lot of pressure to look after my car and brakes, and deal with the conditions. I was trying not to crash into the Safety Car, trying to make sure that no one crashed into me. I could not see out of my mirrors because they were completely fogged up and dirty! My visor was fogged up and had water inside it, so I could not see a thing. I just did the best job I could given the circumstances.'

IT FELT LIKE A FRESH START. The controversy with Ferrari was all over, at last. It was a totally clean slate. I went to Fuji – and it was a good weekend for me all the way through. I started off full of confidence.

Tokyo is eight hours ahead of London and I wanted to be as fit, alert and ready as possible for the Japanese Grand Prix. My fitness team advised me to wake up an hour earlier each day and go to bed earlier each evening while I was still in Europe so I was more used to sleeping at the right time when I got to Japan. I started to do that immediately after I came home from Spa and I also worked hard on my training and my all-round preparations for the races at Fuji and Shanghai.

I was getting up early, going for a run and doing my physical training before most people had breakfast. Towards the end of that week, after the Belgian Grand Prix, I went home to see my family and have a 'Hamilton family' Sunday dinner before leaving for Japan. I felt recharged and focused for whatever lay ahead.

The changes to my sleeping routine helped – I felt a bit less jet-lagged than normal, but not a huge amount. It was still tough to feel completely normal at first when I arrived in Japan but I soon got used to the time difference and just hung out in the capital until we had to go to Fuji. It felt like a long week. Tokyo is a great place, a bit expensive but also a very nice place; it was just that a week was too long for me. I wanted to bring it on. In Tokyo, it was just me and Adam for the first few days, as my dad did not fly out until the following week, just before the race. So I did my training and relaxed and felt as if I just could not wait for that week to pass and for the Grand Prix weekend to come.

I met up with a friend who is from Japan and who I had originally met in London. We visited a few places, took in a couple of good restaurants and a couple of really interesting temples, so that helped take my mind off the racing for a while. It was cool. We were able to just enjoy being in Tokyo, although I was still feeling restless at the same time about wanting to race. The people are so nice in Japan and it is easy to get on and just feel easy. I started to be a bit more adventurous with the food, too, which was a change for me. Normally I am the fussiest person about what I eat (actually, I think Nic is worse than me!), but I am starting to change now because I am travelling to all these places and I want to try new foods. I loved the Japanese tastes – so much so that *teppanyaki* is now my favourite food. I really enjoy it with *wagyu* beef and rice.

After Tokyo, we went to Fuji, which was a pretty cool place, too, considering that all I had to do was look out of my hotel room window and there was Mount Fuji. It was the first volcanic mountain I had ever seen, at least of that height. I just wanted to go and climb it! There was no snow on it, unfortunately, but to get to the circuit from our hotel you had to drive over another mountain, next to Fuji, through the hills and up through the clouds and then back down the other side. It was magnificent. I really enjoyed it. I went there with a very clear mind and I am sure my preparations helped. I felt happy and balanced. I was so confident that I would start with the right set-up, too, after all the homework we did at the factory before I left. I knew I had got it right that time. I knew where I had gone wrong in Spa and that feeling gave me a good boost. So I arrived in Fuji and it was all clear in my mind: I felt that I was potentially in a stronger mental position than Fernando on every level – not just in the car, but also in every kind of way. I just felt great.

At the beginning of the weekend, the press took a couple of things I said and made them sound worse than, or at least quite different from, how they were meant to be. I was quoted as saying that the team wanted me to win and not Fernando, but to the best of my knowledge, I do not believe I ever said that; if I did, then that is not what I would have meant to say or how I should have expressed my view. They asked me if I thought the team favoured me ahead of Fernando and I said, 'No, I don't think they favour either one of us . . . I do not think it has changed anything. The team just wants to win, whether it's me or him . . .'

Perhaps I was a bit naïve, a bit more open than usual with them before that race. It is easy to say the wrong things sometimes and not realize until afterwards that you have said something that can be interpreted in many ways. I see more or less the same group of reporters at each Grand Prix and we have a routine. You have to build up a relationship that works both ways. But this time, I was maybe more open with them, just a little.

They asked me, 'Do you think Fernando has been loyal to the team?' and I said 'No!' I explained why. I should just not have answered, but I did because from what I had heard I did not think he had been loyal. And that was it. It was all I said, but as usual it got expanded into a novel. I do not pay much attention to these things, but obviously everyone reads it or sees it in the end.

All the goings-on throughout this season helped reconfirm in my mind where I wanted to be, with Vodafone McLaren Mercedes. Leading into the weekend, I was mindful of the way Fernando had driven to force me wide off the circuit at the Belgian Grand Prix. I did not want any repeat of that and I did not want us to let things descend into a dangerous battle on the track. I felt that with three races to go and so much at stake, both of us really needed to be careful. We also needed to remind ourselves that we are team-mates. I suppose my overall feeling, in terms of the races ahead, was one of reality about things – I was not going to take any silly risks, I was not going to take anyone off, I was just going to give it my very best shot. In reality, I felt the pressure was all on Fernando. I felt I had nothing to lose and he was the one who was defending the world title.

The weather in Fuji was pretty poor for most of the weekend but it did not stop me taking pole position in qualifying with a late lap that pushed Fernando down to second on the grid. We had fog in the morning and then I left it pretty late in really difficult windy and wet conditions, but I felt I had learned the track well, set the car up nicely and was in the right form at the right time to deliver. It was my fifth career pole in Formula One. The times of the top four from that session show how closely we were matched in terms of sheer speed in qualifying and, therefore, how important each tenth of a second was – it meant that you had to put together a very clean lap with all the corners taken just about perfectly. The lap times were – me first in 1 minute 25.368 seconds, Fernando second with 1:25.438, Kimi third in 1:25.516 and then Felipe fourth with 1:25.765. Nobody else got under 1:26.

Obviously, after that, with Fernando and me on the front row and the Ferraris behind us, the media were keen to talk about the start and the fight at the first corner. We both said that we were keen to avoid any trouble, that we wanted to race hard, fair and square and we both wanted to finish and score points. In all honesty, we both wanted to beat each other and that was apparent, but we both also wanted to survive the first corner. Given the conditions, the high stakes and the tension, it was always going to be an important race and a very important start.

It was not a race without controversy – there did not seem to be too many of them in Formula One this year! There were plenty of incidents and a lot of talk too about how dangerous it was to race in so much rain after running for long periods behind the Safety Car.

The Safety Car was out twice and it was never easy. But I just concentrated and focused completely on bringing the car home in front of everyone else. There was so much rain at the start that the race had to begin behind the Safety Car while everyone waited for the conditions to improve. There was some controversy as well about Ferrari's tyre choice because everyone, except them it seemed, was told to start the race on extreme wets, not intermediates. Ferrari said they had not received the email from Charlie Whiting, the Race Director. It meant Ferrari had to pit after two laps in the rain behind the Safety Car and that really affected their strategy. I was just out there following the Safety Car round and round in the downpour, for 19 laps, and the most important thing was looking after the car in those conditions, staying focused and not making any kind of mistakes.

When we started racing, I was able to pull out a three second lead on Fernando before the first pit stops. Fernando went in first after 27 laps and when he came out he was back in seventh. I pitted a lap later and came out third. We both dropped back a bit while we were running on new tyres with heavy fuel loads. Fernando spun at turn five and was out of the race after his car suffered some body damage in an earlier collision. I was concerned for Fernando when he crashed out. It looked like a nasty accident but eventually I saw him climbing over the safety barriers, so I knew he was okay.

Fernando's departure signalled the arrival of the Safety Car for a second time with me leading ahead of Mark Webber, in his Red Bull, and Sebastian Vettel, who was running third. Then, after 45 of the 67 laps, while we were just trying to see where we were going in all the horrendous spray and rain, Sebastian crashed into the back of Mark's car.

The Safety Car lights were still on, visibility was nil but Mark was right on my tail. I came on the radio and asked my team to request the FIA to ask Mark to back off a little as I felt he was too close to running into the back of my car. I was keen to avoid being crashed into, which is partly why I was out wide.

After the race I heard that Mark blamed Sebastian for the incident. The Stewards investigated the incident and took action against Sebastian and handed out a penalty. Later that week someone complained that I had caused the accident. Of course, I knew none of this at the time because the issue of blame for the accident did not blow up until we arrived in China for the next race.

It felt like the longest race of my life. The conditions were treacherous, it was pouring with rain, visibility was down to almost zero at times and everyone was struggling just to stay on the track. Like everyone else, I had to ride my luck a bit and I was fortunate to continue and to finish the race after Robert Kubica slid into the side of my car, spun me round and nearly out of the race.

I managed to keep everything together to take the win. It was the best and hardest race and win of my career and one of the most exciting. It meant I was now twelve points ahead of Fernando in the championship with two races to go in China and Brazil. It was also my first Formula One victory in the wet, as Phil Prew remarked on the team radio during my slowing down lap. 'We can tick that one off now,' he said. I was just whooping round the track by then!

On the last lap, I remembered some of those great races that Senna and Prost had been involved in and my mind was just rolling these thoughts around . . . this was inspiring but I needed to be disciplined, too. They were my first heroes in Formula One from my early childhood and they had always inspired me and fired my imagination. It was not easy to stop the thoughts of them drifting into my mind at that time. That win in Fuji came after I drove the best race of my life. I out-qualified Fernando in the wet on three laps of heavier fuel and I felt I had put him on the back foot from the first day of the weekend. The win was such a big boost in terms of confidence in my drive to win the World Championship, but at the same time I knew that with two races remaining anything could happen.

I knew I had to knuckle down. I knew I had to stay disciplined. But at the back of my mind, somewhere in the subconscious, I could not stop thinking about it, so I just reminded myself that the key, for me, was to focus on the next race and make sure my preparations were right. I hoped we would have the pace again to create the chance to win. I knew, too, that when pushed to reach a high level to win, I could do it. Afterwards, when a lot of other people went out partying in Tokyo, I just went back to the hotel, had a nice quiet evening with my dad, played pool and relaxed. The next day, Monday, I felt settled, confident and rested, and we flew to Shanghai.

Shanghai is a beautiful city. It is modern, fast, busy, crowded and it has a special buzz. It feels quite amazing with all the lights everywhere and so much going on. You can almost feel the energy. The number of people who live there and who just seem to fill the streets is just ridiculous. I loved that, but I struggled in some other ways – like with the food and the air quality, the heat and the humidity.

We stayed at a hotel about 35 minutes away from the circuit. After the food in Japan, which I loved, I found I was struggling to have a good meal all week in Shanghai even though I really like Chinese food. When I am away like that, I do not like to go out too much. I prefer to stay in the hotel.

In those conditions, when it is so hot and humid, I just want to save all my energy. Travelling from one country to another, from one race to the next, without a break, is pretty stressful. You are away from your friends and family, and your phone does not work . . . I did not have my laptop with me either, so I was not able to get on the internet. I just wanted to chill and do nothing. So, I stored as much energy as I could, doing as little as possible for the next two days, Tuesday and Wednesday.

Then, on Thursday we went to the track and discovered that I was being investigated, all of a sudden, for driving dangerously behind the Safety Car in Fuji. The matter had already been dealt with at the Fuji race meeting, but this was something new. No one had said anything to me after the race or during the week, but obviously a lot was at stake in the Constructors' Championship.

Driving behind the Safety Car in those conditions in a Formula One race was new to me. Like everyone else in that race, I was under a lot of pressure to look after my car and brakes, and deal with the conditions. I was trying not to crash into the Safety Car, trying to make sure that no one crashed into me. I could not see out of my mirrors because they were completely fogged up and dirty! My visor was fogged up and had water inside it, so I could not see a thing. I just did the best job I could given the circumstances.

So, I found myself in front of the Stewards, unusually for events that had happened at a different Grand Prix. Fairness and common sense prevailed in the end but it does not make the process any easier. In view of the conditions in which we were racing, Sebastian's penalty was also removed in relation to the accident involving Mark.

All of this stuff happened when I was supposed to be concentrating and preparing for the race. Going into a race, the momentum starts from the Thursday, but in Shanghai I had to start a new momentum on Saturday morning and that was tough. It just did not seem right.

Saturday arrived, I was still not feeling as good as I had in Fuji, but the weight had been lifted from my shoulders. I was able to get on with my job. I studied the data from practice three, I looked at the onboard footage and I saw where I was losing three-tenths in the last sector. I mapped it out in my head: this is what I have got to do. I went out there for qualifying and it worked. I did what I had hoped to do. I was so happy with myself. I did those corners exactly how I was supposed to and I found the time. Straight away, I was up at the front. In Q1, I was ahead of Fernando; in the second session, I did not do as good a lap and he was quicker than me; in the third session, I just did such a good lap, even looking after my tyres, and the lap was the best I had done all weekend. I got pole position and it could not have been sweeter. The idea was to be out in front and I was. So, all I needed then was to stay out of trouble, stay in front of Fernando, and get to the finish.

I wanted to win the race. When I play golf, and I am in the bushes, I do not play safe. I go for the green. I wanted to race that way but also make sure I finished.

There was a forecast for rain during the race and some people even suggested that I might end up winning the title thanks to a heavy downpour. It was the last thing I wanted, even though I had just won in the wet and I felt confident I could do it again. I really hoped for a dry race. I was not bothered either way, as the car was so good in the rain the previous Sunday, but like most drivers I prefer dry conditions in general. I felt I had gone a long way, through a rollercoaster of a season, to reach that point and I really wanted to win the race in good conditions on the track. I did not want any kind of stoppages to intervene. I suppose, more than anything, I wanted to make the most of being on pole position again.

I was sweet about qualifying, but I had sponsors' appearances to do. I came away from the track at six o'clock and then my driver got lost, so I arrived late for an appearance that I was supposed to do at half past seven. That put me off my rhythm and also I had a bit of a late night – I had to go to another appearance at eight-thirty to nine and then I had to eat. It was not ideal preparation for the most important race of my life. But then, just when I needed a lift, something good happened. My ex-girlfriend Jodia turned up to surprise me. That was a boost that I really did need.

I went to the race the next day and I did not exactly feel perfect. I just cannot deny the fact that I felt I had some pressure on my shoulders. Even if I tell myself that I do not need to think about it and should forget it, it just does not go away.

A special day for Nic.

Above Budapest, Hungarian Grand Prix – waiting patiently for my turn.

Above Imagine the feeling – speechless!

Above A team effort – Vodafone McLaren Mercedes and my family.

Above A difficult time in Turkey but I managed to bring the car home to maintain my championship hopes.

Above Inside Vodafone McLaren Mercedes Brand Centre.

Above My third F1 win – an incredible race in Budapest.

Above A moment of joy with Fernando on the Monza podium.

Above Arriving for the
FIA hearing in Paris.

Right I could hardly see
a thing as I followed the
Safety Car in the rain
and spray.

Right centre 'You beauty!'

Leading from the front.

Above Another great moment of victory to share with my dad after winning in Japan.

Above Family video
– Dad, Linda, Nic
and me.

Right With my
physiotherapist,
personal trainer
and friend Adam
Costanzo.

Comfort and relaxation...

Left Apologizing to Ron Dennis and my team after my retirement in China.

Right One of my young fans – I remember those days well when I used to be one.

Above That moment when I felt gutted in Shanghai – my car beached behind me on the gravel.

Above Diving inside Rubens Barrichello at Brazil as I strived to catch the leaders.

It is one of those things that hangs around in your mind. That feeling of pressure is just there. You cannot get away from it. But I still felt confident, too, like I knew I could do it.

At the start of the race, when I could assess the weather, I knew straightaway that those conditions suited me. I feel I perform well when it is a bit dry and a bit wet. I made a good start, I got clear and I was soon seven-tenths of a second faster than Kimi. I pulled out a nine second gap, then did my first pit stop and I came out ahead. The team were on form.

I thought I was doing my best to race fast and at the same time look after the tyres. I had experience, from way back in karting, of how to look after wet tyres. I was driving through all the wet patches – but the track was drying up. So even though I was being extra careful, the tyres were getting badly worn, especially the right rear which was worn down to the canvas. But because of the conditions and poor visibility I did not even know how bad they were.

Obviously, I knew I was losing my speed. But you cannot feel it from inside the cockpit. I was fighting to keep Kimi behind me and I led the race for 29 laps before he got past. I just could not defend myself anymore. I told the team, 'The tyres are finished. I have to come in soon.' They said, 'You are doing a great job, just stay out for a little bit longer . . .' And, by then, I could see that I was nine seconds off my previous best lap time. Eventually they called me in, and what happened then was something I think I will never forget – it was like a nightmare for me.

I came off the driving line and the pit lane was still very wet. I started turning into the pit lane corner and, without any idea, I just lost the back end. I had okay front tyres, but just no rears at all. I could have braked like ten minutes earlier and really slowed the car down, but I was racing for position. I wasn't to know it was going to be just like an ice-rink and I was going to go off and get stuck in the only gravel trap in a pit lane in the whole world. It was really unfortunate. I tried to avoid the gravel trap, but I was also trying to avoid hitting the wall so I slowed down a little more and the car was just beached. My heart sank. A new rule came out after I was craned back onto the track at the Nürburgring saying that you cannot get lifted back on anymore if you come off the track, so I knew it was over. The team appreciated how I felt. They were not mad. Like me, they were just gutted. We were having a great race and we did not know whether it was going to rain again or not. It was like ice. I could not see in my mirrors, they were completely dirty. I could just feel there was no grip. When I got out of the car, I felt gutted because I had not really made such a mistake all year. To make one then, coming into the pits . . . The team really felt it and I felt their pain and support, too.

Afterwards, I thought – and I hate revisiting this thought – 'Shoot! I was running second, I could have won the race and I was World Champion. For a minute, I was World Champion. Whether I was second, third, fourth, I was going to be World Champion . . .' But at that time, when it happened, I was only thinking as a racer – and that was the mistake I made. It hurt me. My mind ran into overdrive. I needed to keep my head up and I needed to swallow my disappointment. It was not easy for a few minutes, but I did not let my head drop and I did not blame the team. I went to the garage and I shook them all by the hand and I went to the pit wall and did the same. We are a team and it is a team effort through good or bad. The team said they were relying on weather forecasts and wanted to make sure they put me on the best tyres to win the race at the best time. They were hanging on to see what to do, if the weather changed, to avoid making an additional stop. Unfortunately the tyres were finished. I know these things do happen. I felt sorry for the team and I soon pulled myself round. I told them, 'I can still do it, don't worry.'

So I left the circuit and came back home from China that night and kicked myself up the backside a lot, which is something I always do. There was still one race to go. I was still four points in the lead. It wasn't over yet.

I had been leading the championship since race three. Nearly all year! The way I saw it, I had an opportunity and I was going to do my best to take it. The way I felt after that race in Shanghai was the worst feeling ever. Then, in that hour, I learned how it felt to lose a championship, but I realized that I had not lost it. I had just lost that race. I felt the pain. It was a pain I never wanted to experience again. I knew, too, that I still had a great opportunity in Brazil, with a new engine, a car that was still looking very good and a chance to race on a circuit where I could clinch it all. A circuit, too, where the fans had idolized one of my heroes – Ayrton Senna Da Silva. I could not think of a better place to stage the title showdown.

CHAPTER

SAMBA

'The car had just come out of gear. I did not know what had happened. There was just nothing. So I went on the radio and said, 'It's in neutral and it's stopping ...' They said, 'Okay, keep trying to get back in gear' – and I was pulling every lever ...'

IT WAS SUCH A PERFECT BRAZILIAN DAY: great weather, the track was amazing, the circuit full of people – and I was stuck with nothing. No gears, no drive – nothing. My car was just coasting. I lost more than 40 seconds and I was down at the back of the field. I was P18. But I was determined not to give up. I was going to fight all the way to the finish and see what I could do.

By the time we got to São Paulo, I was ready. I felt like this was what I was born for and I was there to do it. All through my career, I had wanted to race in the Brazilian Grand Prix at Interlagos. It has such strong associations with Ayrton Senna, and many great races in the past, and I had heard so much about the place, the city and the circuit that I was really buzzing when I got there.

São Paulo is a vast, sprawling city of more than 20 million inhabitants, but you could feel the vibe of the people and the

atmosphere straight away. They are really friendly and respect-
ful, and they are massive fans of motor racing and Formula
One. I felt at home at once and I just enjoyed the feeling that
here I was, in São Paulo, and I was going to be racing in the
final Grand Prix of the year with a chance of winning the Drivers' Championship in my first season. It felt amazing. I was
just feeling so cool – it was like, 'Yes, bring it on . . .'

I had been preparing for the Brazilian Grand Prix from the
day after we got home from the Chinese race. I relaxed with
my family, played some golf and prepared myself. When my
family went away for a few days on a pre-arranged trip, I was
left to work with Adam on my training programme and I
started to set my body clock for Brazilian time by going to bed
later and getting up later too. I did not have any commitments
for a few days so I was able to chill out. I went to London and
saw some basketball, I hung out with my friends and made
sure I recharged my batteries back at the power station ready
for the final race. It was a cool few days, but they flew by and
in no time we were on the way to the airport to fly out to
Brazil.

We left England on the Monday before the race and it
was nice that my family came with me. I was used to my
dad coming because we go to every race together, but it was
good to have Linda and my brother Nic around when we
arrived and transferred from the airport to the Hilton hotel.
The traffic was something else! The roads were wide and
jammed most of the time, and the whole city just seemed to

hum with cars and people. There was a real sense of anticipation of the race around the city, but I was chilled and
relaxed and I felt good. In some ways, to me, it felt almost
surreal to actually be in Brazil, as for so many years I had
wanted to go there. I had a great reception from the local
people and I felt at home.

We stayed in and relaxed on the Tuesday after arriving,
and I just eased into the pre-race build-up. I wanted to make
everything seem as normal as possible, so it was just like any
other race. I did not want to be talking about the points, the
chances of winning or any of those 'What happens if . . . ?'
scenarios. I knew I was four points ahead of Fernando and
seven in front of Kimi – and if I did my job and finished the
race where I wanted to, then everything would be cool. I had
no doubts in my mind about anything. I felt good about the
team, the hotel and the food. I liked having everyone around
me and I was confident. I was really looking forward to taking
a close look at the track, too, because I had heard and read so
much about it.

The weather was pretty good, too, to start with, but soon
after we arrived it changed. It started raining! I must have
brought it with me from England. After raining for a day or
two it then changed back to being hot again. At least, I
thought, it would give me something to talk about when I
made my sponsors' appearances.

On Wednesday, we had planned to go out as a family and
have a nice, typical Brazilian meal in São Paulo and then in the

afternoon take a trip to the Morumbi Cemetery, which was close by in our part of the city, to visit the grave of Ayrton Senna. Unfortunately, it did not work out – thanks to the paparazzi. As we left the hotel they followed us to the restaurant. While we were eating a really great dish, *feijão com arroz*, which is basically rice and a bean stew, they were sitting outside and when we left they followed us. I cannot say it put me off the food, but it was really disappointing that we were not left alone. We took some detours to try to shake them off and tried all kinds of stuff, but in the end they did not give up and we just had to turn back. The last thing I wanted was to turn my private visit to the Morumbi Cemetery into a media circus and have all my family bothered. I will just have to do it another time.

I put that personal disappointment out of my mind because there were plenty of other things to think about, but it did serve as a reminder of how much my life had changed in such a short space of time. When I thought back to my previous year in GP2, and how free I was to travel around and do my own thing, I realized that it would not be the same again. You just have to keep making personal-life adjustments if you are a Formula One driver and it is not easy. There is no textbook to tell you what to do next! I think we were all a bit disappointed about that afternoon, but we knew we were in Brazil for the Grand Prix – we were determined to keep smiling and go on and do our utmost.

After all this, I was glad to go to the circuit for the first time and take a look at it on Thursday. This was the place I had heard a lot about, not only from my great personal interest in Ayrton Senna but also from other drivers like Felipe, who was born in São Paulo. So, too, was Rubens Barrichello. It is a circuit with a special history for Formula One and although the facilities were not ideal, because they are so cramped, the actual track is really challenging and special for a driver. The surface had been completely redone this year, so it was much smoother and a lot of the famous old bumps were gone. It is an anti-clockwise track, which means a lot of strain on the left side of your neck, instead of the right, as most circuits are clockwise. I had been doing extra fitness work with Adam to build up my neck muscles to help cope with that and I could see, from the first corner, that I was going to need it. From the start, there is a straight and then a left-hand corner that drops away and descends through an S-bend, named after Senna, into the outfield. The track has a lot of gradient changes, too, and a climb back up to the right-hander that leads back onto the straight. I could see that it was a demanding and challenging place, but I relished that challenge. After all I had heard about it, it was living up to expectations!

Before I went out to walk the track, we had a press conference attended by myself, Fernando, Felipe and Kimi. The room was packed, there were cameras and lights all around, and it was impossible not to feel the pressure and tension in the air. There was a lot of interest in me, because of the World Championship, of course, but also in the England rugby team's chances in the World Cup final that was taking place in Paris on the Saturday. I said they had done a fantastic job to reach the final and wished them all the best. There were a few questions, too, about the FIA's decision to appoint an observer to be in our garage for the weekend and, as usual, some about me and Fernando.

I was glad to be into the routine of the weekend, getting nearer to going out on the track in the car for the first time and concentrating on my job. The whole of the build-up to the race was there around me and I was buzzing. It is always cool to get support from fans all over the world, but I did feel something extra about being in São Paulo with the Brazilian fans. That evening, I was asked to attend and answer some questions at an event organized by the team's sponsor Johnnie Walker and, apart from talking about responsible drinking, I was given a great opportunity to listen to some of the local people talking about their love of motor racing and Formula One. I said, 'I was in my room just now and looking out of the window, thinking "Wow! Last year I was GP2 champion and I was hoping I would be in Formula One this year – I remember discussing with McLaren the possibility of me doing this race last year – and now I am here. I am experienced, I have been competitive all year and leading the championship – it is just crazy. I cannot believe it – I am simply stunned."' That was pretty much how I felt. I am only 22 and I was there talking about racing for the World Championship in Brazil.

It was, of course, not the first time a championship had been settled in Brazil; nor was it the first time that three drivers had gone into the last race with a chance of winning. But it had been a long time. Enough people had come by and talked to me about the last time, when Nigel Mansell had a tyre blow-out in Adelaide in 1986, so I got the message . . . but I think they forgot I was only a one-year-old baby at the time! There were so many talking points, but I just tried to stay out of the way, store my energy and concentrate on the task.

I went to bed that Thursday night feeling good. I had a room with a view over the river and a great sense of anticipation. The next morning, when I woke up, it was raining steadily -- which meant that my first time out on the circuit in practice was going to be in wet conditions. I am a quick and confident learner on any new circuit, and Interlagos had always been one of my favourites so I was not too worried. I knew where the track went and what to expect, but it is always more difficult to do the job properly in the wet. It was pretty tricky out there in the first morning session and I did ten laps to learn my way around while Fernando did just one installation lap.

In the afternoon, it was much drier and Fernando did 28 laps in all and I did 27, clocking a best time of one minute and 12.767, one-tenth of a second quicker than Fernando's best. That was sweet for me. It was so important to be faster than my team-mate and prove I was enjoying the track which, in the afternoon, was great to drive on. It was an amazing experience. I got a good feel for the circuit, managed to make some progress with the set-up work and also did some decent work on tyre comparisons despite the cold and wet conditions. So I felt we did well – except for one small mistake where we used one set of wet tyres too many during the morning session. The rule about wet tyres had changed recently and it was just one of those things.

We did not gain any advantage from it at all, as I only used them to carry out one installation lap, but we were fined 15,000 Euros and had to give back one set of wet weather tyres. Two other teams made the same mistake and had to do the same thing for a similar infringement of the rules. It was not controversial, just an error. Ron suggested to the media that perhaps the team were trying too hard and said it was a 'silly mistake' that showed everyone is human. And that was it. It was a small thing, the team were doing a fantastic job and we just needed to keep pushing, get on with it and get the job done. It was not the end of the world. I had still topped the times ahead of Fernando at the end of my first day's practice in the rain at Interlagos. I was happy with that. Felipe was third and Kimi was fourth and, that evening, it seemed as if we might have the edge, though I knew the Ferraris were going to be fast.

I went back to the hotel and chilled out, ate and slept well. It was cool to have Nic around and feel my family there in support. I wanted to be at my best for qualifying the next day. When I woke up, I felt good, the weather was better, much warmer with sunshine, and when we got to the track the whole place was humming. The atmosphere was really buzzing, like me, and I could not wait for qualifying in the afternoon. Both Q1 and Q2 went fine and I was right at the front of the queue in the pit lane for Q3 when the fight for pole began. For me, it was about making sure the car worked well, burning off the fuel and putting in a really good final lap. Obviously, it was the same for all of us and there was clearly a high level of tension with Ferrari trying to take the drivers' title with Kimi, and Fernando using all of his experience to beat him – and me.

I knew it was important to take pole, if I could, but the main thing for me was to be up the front. It was not the end of the world if I qualified third, or fourth. I just had to be up the front. We had the pace in the car, I felt sure of that. And though I wanted to win, I knew that I did not have to in order to take the championship. I took the view that I would drive to win, because that is the only way I really know how to approach a race, but I knew that if I could not beat the other guys then I could finish behind them and still do the job. There were enough other people working out the points I needed for me not to worry about it. But it was not my ambition to start the race aiming to finish fourth, so I was gunning for pole.

It was a really close session in qualifying – very, very close and I enjoyed it! I ended up second, just behind Felipe who had the extra speed you get sometimes from racing in front of your home crowd. I felt like we had good pace, the car was great to drive and the team did a superb job, as always, in making sure I was out in good space. My fastest timed lap was also really good, but I lost a little time in the last corner. It was close to a perfect lap and I felt comfortable about everything. It was tense for everyone in the team, of course, to have two cars racing for the championship, but they did a great job in making sure we both had the extra lap. To be honest, pole would have been perfect, but I was focused on the job ahead, winning the championship, and that was the main prize.

We only had one pit crew working for the session, so that meant Fernando and I had some stacked pit stops when I came in first and Fernando was right behind me. I got my tyres on and pushed hard to get out as soon as possible to make sure Fernando could get his tyres and get out, too. It worked perfectly each time.

For me, the main thing was that I was happy. The car felt great underneath me in that session and, in dry conditions for the first time, I loved the circuit. I saw some British flags out there in the middle of the Brazilian fans. They were really enthusiastic, and I was glad of the support. Second on the grid, on the left side, meant starting on the dirtier part of the track, but I was not worried.

Once qualifying was over, there was a special event in the paddock for most people to go and watch – the Rugby World Cup final between England and South Africa – and as soon as I was free of my commitments I went back to the team's hospitality area to see the match. It was broadcast live from Paris, we had English commentary and for an hour or two I could submerge myself in another great sport and enjoy a world-class contest surrounded by friends and team-members. We were all – or nearly all – rooting for England over there in Interlagos, but it was not quite enough.

Next morning, as soon as I looked outside, I could see it was a hot day. There was not a cloud in the sky, the air was clear and the sun was climbing high. There were crowds at the circuit gates and there was a real sense of anticipation inside. Most of the seats in the grandstands around the track were filled by ten o'clock in the morning, four hours before the race, and there was a kind of carnival atmosphere. Obviously, a lot of the crowd supported Felipe, because he had won the year before and he was their local hero, but I felt like I had good support, too. The paddock was over-crowded and you could hardly move for people, television crews, crowds gathered around visitors and celebrities, and all the normal chaos in the build-up to a Grand Prix. When I went to the bathroom, there were photographers waiting for me to come out! It was that kind of crazy.

We tried our best in the team to make it as normal as possible for us all. Fernando and I both did the usual Paddock Club appearances, we went on the Drivers' Parade and we went to eat at the same time as usual. I was enjoying it all. When we started the pre-race routine, there were people all around the garage exit, and it was difficult to see out, but once things were cleared it was fine. The atmosphere was just crackling.

On the grid, again it was packed with photographers, media and guests. I just did my best to stay cool, out of the way, under a parasol with my dad and chill out and concentrate on the race. I could not wait for it to begin. I knew I needed to make a good start if I could. Unfortunately, when the lights went out, I did not make a great start at all and Felipe was able to pull away into the lead followed by Kimi, who came past me from third. I just did not get the speed and as we went into the first corner I could see Fernando pulling alongside me, on the outside. I tried to defend myself, but he had the line as we turned down and into the second part of the Senna turn. We were very close.

All my competitive instincts took control as we raced down through the long left-hand Curva do Sol and into the outfield straight. I did not want to drop from second to fourth or to let Fernando run in front of me. As we approached the sharp left-hand Subida do Lago corner, under-braking, I tried to find a way past Fernando on the outside again, this time on the slippery area, but locked up to avoid hitting him as he defended – and I ran off. By the time I had recovered and rejoined I was down in eighth. To anyone watching and supporting me it must have looked like a disaster.

I knew it was bad, but I also knew there was a long way to go and it was not an irretrievable position. I had done it before. I knew I had a great car. I felt quite relaxed. I had the pace to reclaim my position. So I set about climbing back into the top group as soon as I could. I think I passed Jarno Trulli on lap 2 to get up to seventh and then passed Nick Heidfeld on lap 7 before the next setback – that difficult moment when I was left with a fistful of nothing in the gearbox on lap 8. Shoot! Just when I needed some good luck, I was getting all my bad luck in one race. The car lost its drive and I was stuck in neutral, just coasting as I downshifted going into turn four, the Subida da Lago, again. In a flash, I could see everything passing me – all the other cars, the whole season, everything we had done.

The car had just come out of gear. I did not know what had happened. There was just nothing. So I went on the radio and said, 'It's in neutral and it's stopping . . .' They said, 'Okay, keep trying to get back in gear' – and I was pulling every lever, I wouldn't say in a panic, but at the same time it was like 'Bugger!' and people were going by me, passing me, all those cars and it was like my life was flashing past. Eventually, the car just came to a halt because going uphill there was nothing to drive it, but the engine kept ticking over. Luckily I got the hydraulics back and it engaged again. Phew! I was back in seventh gear – so the anti-stall cut in – and then I had to shift back down through all the gears to find first, start again and rejoin the race.

We had had such a phenomenal reliability record all season and now the gremlins wanted to come and play. I knew I had to try to stay calm and concentrate on following instructions to regain some gears. I was so relieved. I was able to get going again. But from then on, I had to manage the engine, so I was running on quite low revs.

On another day, I might have enjoyed it, as I fought through the field. I passed Rubens Barrichello and Adrian Sutil on laps 11 and 12, and then Ralf Schumacher, Anthony Davidson and Takuma Sato on lap 15. I felt like I was fighting for positions all the time and passing cars on every lap. The team went for a three-stop strategy. It was a pretty bold, radical move that meant I was running lighter and on the better tyres at the end of the race, but it also meant an extra pit stop. I stopped on laps 22, 36 and 56. And when Kimi took the lead after passing Felipe during the second pit stops, I knew it was going to be very difficult to finish in the top five – and that's what I really needed to do.

I did my best. I drove as hard as I could – and set the fastest lap at that time in the race almost immediately after my third stop – and in the end I finished seventh. I needed more time, but the race and its 71 laps ran out on me. I never stopped pushing, I really just kept trying as hard as I could to the end. I knew we were not as fast as the Ferraris because of the way we were running our engine, but we were as fast as anyone else. I just kept my belief going and kept pushing all the way to the chequered flag.

The Ferraris were out on their own and they came home first and second, Kimi ahead of Felipe. Fernando was third and then it was my old karting team-mate Nico Rosberg, fourth for Williams, ahead of the two BMWs of Robert Kubica and Nick

Heidfeld. Kimi had won the drivers' title for the first time, just a few days after his 28th birthday. He drove a brilliant race and I was pleased for him. In the end, he finished with 110 points to be champion and I had 109, the same as Fernando. But I was runner-up in the championship because, although Fernando and I had scored four wins each, I had scored more second places.

When I got out of the car at the end of the race, David Coulthard was parked alongside me. 'Did you win?' he asked. 'What happened?' I told him about the gearbox failure and then we walked to the garage and applauded the two Ferraris and I shook Kimi's hand and said well done to him, congratulations. Then I went back to the Vodafone McLaren Mercedes garage and shook hands with everyone in the team, thanking them for all their effort throughout the season. I wouldn't say I was gutted. I felt the same as I did at the start of the race – relaxed. At the garage, we were all disappointed . . . but, you know, this is racing. The team did a phenomenal job and I said that to everyone. Then I went and gave Linda a hug and she said she was so proud of me, and I saw Nic – he is so very strong and supportive of me. Ron said he was sorry. I said to him, 'Ron, thank you for an amazing year and thanks for the opportunity you gave me and for sticking by me for all this time – and we'll do it next year!'

To finish second at the end of my first season, as a rookie, in Formula One was certainly no failure, but I could not deny I felt a sense of disappointment to have gone so close to taking the title. I was four points ahead at the start of the day and suffered mechanical problems and bad luck at the wrong time. It was not a sweet moment! But I had to take the positives from it and look ahead to 2008.

EARLY RACE CAREER

1995 (aged 10)
Formula Cadets
Super 1 Series Champion
STP Superprix Champion

1996
Formula Cadets
McLaren Mercedes Champions of the Future Champion
UK 5 Nations Champion
SKT TV Kart Masters Champion

1997
Formula Junior Yamaha
McLaren Mercedes Champions of the Future Champion
Super 1 Series British Champion

1998
Formula Junior Intercontinental 'A'
McLaren Mercedes Champions of the Future runner-up

1999
Formula Junior Intercontinental 'A'
Vico European Champion
Italian Trophy de Pomposa Champion

Formula Junior Intercontinental 'A'
Italian Industrials Champion

2000
Formula 'A'
European Champion
World Cup Champion
Elf Masters Champion
Ranked World No.1 in the Champion Kart driver rankings
British Racing Driver Club rising star member

2001
Formula Renault UK Winter Series – *Manor Motorsport*
Fifth in championship

2002
Formula Renault UK Championship – *Manor Motorsport*
Third in championship with three race wins; three pole positions and three fastest laps

Formula Renault EuroCup Championship
Fifth in championship with one win

2003
Formula Renault UK Championship – *Manor Motorsport*
Champion with 10 wins, 11 pole positions and 9 fastest laps

2004
F3 Euroseries – *Manor Motorsport*
Fifth in championship with one race win
Winner of Bahrain F3 Superprix

2005
F3 Euroseries – *ASM F3*
Champion with 15 wins, 13 pole positions and 10 fastest laps
Winner of F3 Masters

2006
GP2 series – *ART Grand Prix*
Champion with five wins, six fastest laps and pole position at Monaco

2007 FORMULA ONE RESULTS

Australian Grand Prix
16–18 March 2007

Kimi Räikkönen takes pole position and then produces an inspired win in Melbourne. As Räikkönen streaks to victory, the other podium places go to his former team, McLaren Mercedes. Double World Champion Fernando Alonso is second, ahead of 22-year-old Lewis Hamilton. Hamilton impresses in his first Formula One race: his third place is the best debut finish by an Englishman since 1966. The highlight of the race is Hamilton flying off the second row of the grid and beating Alonso to the first corner. Hamilton stays in front of Alonso for 42 laps but yields when the champion is able to stay out for two laps longer on his second stint and Hamilton is held up by the Super Aguri of Takuma Sato on his way into the pits. Felipe Massa takes sixth despite a gearbox failure in qualifying.

LEWIS: 'I braked. I do not even know how I judged where I was, braking-wise. And then, there was a gap around the outside of Fernando! I just slotted in so perfectly.'

QUALIFYING

Pos	No	Driver	Team	Q1	Q2	Q3
1	6	Kimi Räikkönen	Ferrari	1:26.644	1:25.644	1:26.072
2	1	Fernando Alonso	McLaren Mercedes	1:26.697	1:25.326	1:26.493
3	9	Nick Heidfeld	BMW-Sauber	1:26.895	1:25.358	1:26.556
4	2	Lewis Hamilton	McLaren Mercedes	1:26.674	1:25.577	1:26.755
5	10	Robert Kubica	BMW-Sauber	1:26.696	1:25.882	1:27.347
6	3	Giancarlo Fisichella	Renault	1:27.270	1:25.944	1:27.634
7	15	Mark Webber	Red Bull-Renault	1:26.978	1:26.623	1:27.934
8	12	Jarno Trulli	Toyota	1:27.014	1:26.688	1:28.404
9	11	Ralf Schumacher	Toyota	1:27.328	1:26.739	1:28.692
10	22	Takuma Sato	Super Aguri-Honda	1:27.365	1:26.758	1:28.871

RACE

Pos	No	Driver	Team	Laps	Time/Retired	Grid	Pts
1	6	Kimi Räikkönen	Ferrari	58	1:25:28.770	1	10
2	1	Fernando Alonso	McLaren Mercedes	58	+7.2 secs	2	8
3	2	Lewis Hamilton	McLaren Mercedes	58	+18.5 secs	4	6
4	9	Nick Heidfeld	BMW-Sauber	58	+38.7 secs	3	5
5	3	Giancarlo Fisichella	Renault	58	+66.4 secs	6	4
6	5	Felipe Massa	Ferrari	58	+66.8 secs	22	3
7	16	Nico Rosberg	Williams-Toyota	57	+1 Lap	12	2
8	11	Ralf Schumacher	Toyota	57	+1 Lap	9	1
9	12	Jarno Trulli	Toyota	57	+1 Lap	8	
10	4	Heikki Kovalainen	Renault	57	+1 Lap	13	

Fastest lap: Kimi Räikkönen, Ferrari: 1:25.235

Malaysian Grand Prix

6–8 April 2007

In Sepang, Ferrari's Felipe Massa bounces back from the disappointment of Melbourne to take pole position in qualifying. A pulsating final lap earns his place in front of Alonso and Räikkönen. Hamilton again qualifies strongly in fourth. In the race, Vodafone McLaren Mercedes sensationally claim the first one-two of the season, with Alonso leading Hamilton to the chequered flag. Hamilton starts superbly, overtaking both Ferraris and moving into second place behind Alonso who had passed Massa at the first corner. Massa overtakes Hamilton on the third lap but the rookie is able to quickly reclaim second place. This particular battle ends on the sixth lap when Massa makes a desperate attempt to overtake Hamilton and ends up sliding off the track. Thereafter, Hamilton holds off a sustained attack from Räikkönen, allowing Alonso to proceed to victory. Alonso leads the Drivers' Championship on 18 points, ahead of Räikkönen on 16 and Hamilton on 14.

LEWIS: 'Felipe made a couple of moves to pass me, into turn four, I think. I was lucky because I was able to lead him into a mistake ...'

QUALIFYING

Pos	No	Driver	Team	Q1	Q2	Q3
1	5	Felipe Massa	Ferrari	1:35.340	1:34.454	1:35.043
2	1	Fernando Alonso	McLaren Mercedes	1:34.942	1:34.057	1:35.310
3	6	Kimi Räikkönen	Ferrari	1:35.138	1:34.687	1:35.479
4	2	Lewis Hamilton	McLaren Mercedes	1:35.028	1:34.650	1:36.045
5	9	Nick Heidfeld	BMW-Sauber	1:35.617	1:35.203	1:36.543
6	16	Nico Rosberg	Williams-Toyota	1:35.755	1:35.380	1:36.829
7	10	Robert Kubica	BMW-Sauber	1:35.294	1:34.739	1:36.896
8	12	Jarno Trulli	Toyota	1:35.666	1:35.255	1:36.902
9	11	Ralf Schumacher	Toyota	1:35.736	1:35.595	1:37.078
10	15	Mark Webber	Red Bull-Renault	1:35.727	1:35.579	1:37.345

RACE

Pos	No	Driver	Team	Laps	Time/Retired	Grid	Pts
1	1	Fernando Alonso	McLaren Mercedes	56	1:32:14.930	2	10
2	2	Lewis Hamilton	McLaren Mercedes	56	+17.5 secs	4	8
3	6	Kimi Räikkönen	Ferrari	56	+18.3 secs	3	6
4	9	Nick Heidfeld	BMW-Sauber	56	+33.7 secs	5	5
5	5	Felipe Massa	Ferrari	56	+36.7 secs	1	4
6	3	Giancarlo Fisichella	Renault	56	+65.6 secs	12	3
7	12	Jarno Trulli	Toyota	56	+70.1 secs	8	2
8	4	Heikki Kovalainen	Renault	56	+72.0 secs	11	1
9	17	Alexander Wurz	Williams-Toyota	56	+89.9 secs	19	
10	15	Mark Webber	Red Bull-Renault	56	+93.5 secs	10	

Fastest lap: Lewis Hamilton, Vodafone McLaren Mercedes: 1:36.701

Bahrain Grand Prix

13–15 April 2007

In qualifying, Massa takes his second consecutive pole position and Hamilton is just behind in second, his best starting grid position to date. During the race, Massa manages to hold on for his first win of the season despite Hamilton applying pressure early and late in the contest. The Brazilian makes no mistakes, however, and Hamilton is forced to settle for second. He still snatches the headlines, though, as he becomes the first rookie to finish on the podium in his first three races. Ferrari's Kimi Räikkönen is third, ahead of BMW's Nick Heidfeld defending well to resist a challenge from Alonso who endures a testing weekend in the Vodafone McLaren Mercedes. The result leaves Hamilton, Alonso and Räikkönen in a three-way tie on points at the top of the world standings. Massa is five points adrift.

LEWIS: 'After that, it was just me and Felipe in front, and we had a really close scrap, but I just could not find a way to get near enough to pass him.'

QUALIFYING

Pos	No	Driver	Team	Q1	Q2	Q3
1	5	Felipe Massa	Ferrari	1:32.443	1:31.359	1:32.652
2	2	Lewis Hamilton	McLaren Mercedes	1:32.580	1:31.732	1:32.935
3	6	Kimi Räikkönen	Ferrari	1:33.161	1:31.812	1:33.131
4	1	Fernando Alonso	McLaren Mercedes	1:33.049	1:32.214	1:33.192
5	9	Nick Heidfeld	BMW-Sauber	1:33.164	1:32.154	1:33.404
6	10	Robert Kubica	BMW-Sauber	1:33.348	1:32.292	1:33.710
7	3	Giancarlo Fisichella	Renault	1:33.556	1:32.889	1:34.056
8	15	Mark Webber	Red Bull-Renault	1:33.496	1:32.800	1:34.106
9	12	Jarno Trulli	Toyota	1:33.210	1:32.429	1:34.154
10	16	Nico Rosberg	Williams-Toyota	1:33.349	1:32.815	1:34.399

RACE

Pos	No	Driver	Team	Laps	Time/Retired	Grid	Pts
1	5	Felipe Massa	Ferrari	57	1:33:27.515	1	10
2	2	Lewis Hamilton	McLaren Mercedes	57	+2.3 secs	2	8
3	6	Kimi Räikkönen	Ferrari	57	+10.8 secs	3	6
4	9	Nick Heidfeld	BMW-Sauber	57	+13.8 secs	5	5
5	1	Fernando Alonso	McLaren Mercedes	57	+14.4 secs	4	4
6	10	Robert Kubica	BMW-Sauber	57	+45.5 secs	6	3
7	12	Jarno Trulli	Toyota	57	+81.3 secs	9	2
8	3	Giancarlo Fisichella	Renault	57	+81.7 secs	7	1
9	4	Heikki Kovalainen	Renault	57	+89.4 secs	12	
10	16	Nico Rosberg	Williams-Toyota	57	+89.9 secs	10	

Fastest lap: Felipe Massa, Ferrari: 1:34.067

Spanish Grand Prix

11–13 May 2007

Vodafone McLaren Mercedes are fastest throughout practice but cannot carry their speed advantage into qualifying. Massa is fractionally faster than Alonso and claims pole. Hamilton is fourth on the grid behind Räikkönen. In a dazzling first lap on race day, Hamilton passes Alonso and Räikkönen to take second place where he eventually finishes, once again behind the excellent Massa. Alonso pays the price for an audacious attempt to overtake Massa at the first corner. Their two cars touch, forcing Alonso off the track momentarily. The Spaniard rejoins the race in fourth position and eventually finishes third, after Räikkönen retires with a technical problem. At 22 years, four months and six days, Hamilton is the youngest driver in history to lead the Drivers' Championship outright. He has 30 points, ahead of Alonso on 28 and Massa on 27.

LEWIS: 'I couldn't catch him [Massa], but importantly for me, I stayed in front of Fernando … I was leading the championship. That was sweet.'

QUALIFYING

Pos	No	Driver	Team	Q1	Q2	Q3
1	5	Felipe Massa	Ferrari	1:21.375	1:20.597	1:21.421
2	1	Fernando Alonso	McLaren Mercedes	1:21.609	1:20.797	1:21.451
3	6	Kimi Räikkönen	Ferrari	1:21.802	1:20.741	1:21.723
4	2	Lewis Hamilton	McLaren Mercedes	1:21.120	1:20.713	1:21.785
5	10	Robert Kubica	BMW-Sauber	1:21.941	1:21.381	1:22.253
6	12	Jarno Trulli	Toyota	1:22.501	1:21.554	1:22.324
7	9	Nick Heidfeld	BMW-Sauber	1:21.625	1:21.113	1:22.389
8	4	Heikki Kovalainen	Renault	1:21.790	1:21.623	1:22.568
9	14	David Coulthard	Red Bull-Renault	1:22.491	1:21.488	1:22.749
10	3	Giancarlo Fisichella	Renault	1:22.064	1:21.677	1:22.881

RACE

Pos	No	Driver	Team	Laps	Time/Retired	Grid	Pts
1	5	Felipe Massa	Ferrari	65	1:31:36.230	1	10
2	2	Lewis Hamilton	McLaren Mercedes	65	+6.7 secs	4	8
3	1	Fernando Alonso	McLaren Mercedes	65	+17.4 secs	2	6
4	10	Robert Kubica	BMW-Sauber	65	+31.6 secs	5	5
5	14	David Coulthard	Red Bull-Renault	65	+58.3 secs	9	4
6	16	Nico Rosberg	Williams-Toyota	65	+59.5 secs	11	3
7	4	Heikki Kovalainen	Renault	65	+62.1 secs	8	2
8	22	Takuma Sato	Super Aguri-Honda	64	+1 Lap	13	1
9	3	Giancarlo Fisichella	Renault	64	+1 Lap	10	
10	8	Rubens Barrichello	Honda	64	+1 Lap	12	

Fastest lap: Felipe Massa, Ferrari: 1:22.680

Monaco Grand Prix

24–27 May 2007

In qualifying, Alonso takes pole position, less than two-tenths of a second quicker than Hamilton. The Vodafone McLaren Mercedes exploit their front row grid positions in the race, Alonso moving to the top of the championship with a victory and Hamilton finishing second. At one point during the race, Hamilton appears to be cutting the gap on his team-mate but falls away again and Vodafone McLaren Mercedes take their second one-two finish of the season. Afterwards, the processional nature of the race causes the FIA to launch an enquiry into the possibility of illegal team orders denying Hamilton the chance to challenge Alonso. After much deliberation, the first controversy of the season ends with the FIA clearing Vodafone McLaren Mercedes of the charge. Alonso and Hamilton now both have 38 championship points, but the Spaniard's two wins put him top. Massa, who finished third in Monaco, is also third in the championship with 33 points.

LEWIS: 'I stuck behind him [Alonso] to the end. After the race it was evident my team were not happy, but I said, "I'm not here to finish second."'

QUALIFYING

Pos	No	Driver	Team	Q1	Q2	Q3
1	1	Fernando Alonso	McLaren Mercedes	1:16.059	1:15.431	1:15.726
2	2	Lewis Hamilton	McLaren Mercedes	1:15.685	1:15.479	1:15.905
3	5	Felipe Massa	Ferrari	1:16.786	1:16.034	1:15.967
4	3	Giancarlo Fisichella	Renault	1:17.596	1:16.054	1:16.285
5	16	Nico Rosberg	Williams-Toyota	1:16.870	1:16.100	1:16.439
6	15	Mark Webber	Red Bull-Renault	1:17.816	1:16.420	1:16.784
7	9	Nick Heidfeld	BMW-Sauber	1:17.385	1:15.733	1:16.832
8	10	Robert Kubica	BMW-Sauber	1:17.504	1:15.576	1:16.955
9	8	Rubens Barrichello	Honda	1:17.244	1:16.454	1:17.498
10	7	Jenson Button	Honda	1:17.297	1:16.457	1:17.939

RACE

Pos	No	Driver	Team	Laps	Time/Retired	Grid	Pts
1	1	Fernando Alonso	McLaren Mercedes	78	1:40:29.329	1	10
2	2	Lewis Hamilton	McLaren Mercedes	78	+4.0 secs	2	8
3	5	Felipe Massa	Ferrari	78	+69.1 secs	3	6
4	3	Giancarlo Fisichella	Renault	77	+1 Lap	4	5
5	10	Robert Kubica	BMW-Sauber	77	+1 Lap	8	4
6	9	Nick Heidfeld	BMW-Sauber	77	+1 Lap	7	3
7	17	Alexander Wurz	Williams-Toyota	77	+1 Lap	11	2
8	6	Kimi Räikkönen	Ferrari	77	+1 Lap	16	1
9	19	Scott Speed	STR-Ferrari	77	+1 Lap	18	
10	8	Rubens Barrichello	Honda	77	+1 Lap	9	

Fastest lap: Fernando Alonso, Vodafone McLaren Mercedes: 1:15.284

Canadian Grand Prix

8–10 June 2007

Hamilton's maiden Formula One pole position is secured at a circuit he has never raced on before. In a reversal of their qualifying performance in Monaco, Alonso joins Hamilton on the front row. Then, as his main rivals falter, Hamilton cruises to his first Formula One victory, ahead of Nick Heidfeld and Alexander Wurz. The race is notable for four Safety Car interventions and a high-speed crash involving BMW's Robert Kubica. Alonso finishes seventh after an eventful race, losing second place to Heidfeld at the first corner and then dropping to thirteenth after a ten-second penalty for making an enforced pit stop in a Safety Car period. Räikkönen is fifth for Ferrari and Massa is disqualified for leaving the pits when the pit lane exit was closed. Hamilton moves to 48 points in the championship, with Alonso on 40 and Massa on 33.

LEWIS: 'Each time the Safety Car came out, I was thinking "Uh-oh, someone doesn't want you to win this" … It did not get to me, though. I thought it was a good challenge – and it kept me busy.'

QUALIFYING

Pos	No	Driver	Team	Q1	Q2	Q3
1	2	Lewis Hamilton	McLaren Mercedes	1:16.576	1:15.486	1:15.707
2	1	Fernando Alonso	McLaren Mercedes	1:16.562	1:15.522	1:16.163
3	9	Nick Heidfeld	BMW-Sauber	1:17.006	1:15.960	1:16.266
4	6	Kimi Räikkönen	Ferrari	1:16.468	1:16.592	1:16.411
5	5	Felipe Massa	Ferrari	1:16.756	1:16.138	1:16.570
6	15	Mark Webber	Red Bull-Renault	1:17.315	1:16.257	1:16.913
7	16	Nico Rosberg	Williams-Toyota	1:17.016	1:16.190	1:16.919
8	10	Robert Kubica	BMW-Sauber	1:17.267	1:16.368	1:16.993
9	3	Giancarlo Fisichella	Renault	1:16.805	1:16.288	1:17.229
10	12	Jarno Trulli	Toyota	1:17.324	1:16.600	1:17.747

RACE

Pos	No	Driver	Team	Laps	Time/Retired	Grid	Pts
1	2	Lewis Hamilton	McLaren Mercedes	70	1:44:11.292	1	10
2	9	Nick Heidfeld	BMW-Sauber	70	+4.3 secs	3	8
3	17	Alexander Wurz	Williams-Toyota	70	+5.3 secs	19	6
4	4	Heikki Kovalainen	Renault	70	+6.7 secs	22	5
5	6	Kimi Räikkönen	Ferrari	70	+13.0 secs	4	4
6	22	Takuma Sato	Super Aguri-Honda	70	+16.6 secs	11	3
7	1	Fernando Alonso	McLaren Mercedes	70	+21.9 secs	2	2
8	11	Ralf Schumacher	Toyota	70	+22.8 secs	18	1
9	15	Mark Webber	Red Bull-Renault	70	+22.9 secs	6	
10	16	Nico Rosberg	Williams-Toyota	70	+23.9 secs	7	

Fastest lap: Fernando Alonso, Vodafone McLaren Mercedes: 1:16.367

United States Grand Prix

15–17 June 2007

The Indianapolis Motor Speedway is another track that Hamilton has never driven before but in qualifying he takes his second pole position in eight days. Again, Alonso is second on the grid, unable to match the pace of his team-mate. On race day, Hamilton wins from the front for the second consecutive race. Alonso makes one desperate attempt to pass and manages to pull alongside Hamilton on lap 39. The Spaniard seems destined for the lead but after some stubborn Hamilton defending, the World Champion is forced to settle for second place. Felipe Massa is a distant third for Ferrari and Räikkönen is fourth, while BMW's 19-year-old Sebastian Vettel becomes the youngest ever Formula One point scorer. Vettel, standing in for Robert Kubica, takes eighth place in his debut race. Hamilton, whose run of podium finishes now stretches to seven races, has 58 World Championship points. Alonso has 48 and Massa 39.

LEWIS: 'At one point, we did battle almost literally wheel-to-wheel, but he [Alonso] was not coming past. I am no pushover – if anything, I am one of the hardest drivers to overtake ...'

QUALIFYING

Pos	No	Driver	Team	Q1	Q2	Q3
1	2	Lewis Hamilton	McLaren Mercedes	1:12.563	1:12.065	1:12.331
2	1	Fernando Alonso	McLaren Mercedes	1:12.416	1:11.926	1:12.500
3	5	Felipe Massa	Ferrari	1:12.731	1:12.180	1:12.703
4	6	Kimi Räikkönen	Ferrari	1:12.732	1:12.111	1:12.839
5	9	Nick Heidfeld	BMW-Sauber	1:12.543	1:12.188	1:12.847
6	4	Heikki Kovalainen	Renault	1:12.998	1:12.599	1:13.308
7	10	Sebastian Vettel	BMW-Sauber	1:12.711	1:12.644	1:13.513
8	12	Jarno Trulli	Toyota	1:13.186	1:12.828	1:13.789
9	15	Mark Webber	Red Bull-Renault	1:13.425	1:12.788	1:13.871
10	3	Giancarlo Fisichella	Renault	1:13.168	1:12.603	1:13.953

RACE

Pos	No	Driver	Team	Laps	Time/Retired	Grid	Pts
1	2	Lewis Hamilton	McLaren Mercedes	73	1:31:09.965	1	10
2	1	Fernando Alonso	McLaren Mercedes	73	+1.5 secs	2	8
3	5	Felipe Massa	Ferrari	73	+12.8 secs	3	6
4	6	Kimi Räikkönen	Ferrari	73	+15.4 secs	4	5
5	4	Heikki Kovalainen	Renault	73	+41.4 secs	6	4
6	12	Jarno Trulli	Toyota	73	+66.7 secs	8	3
7	15	Mark Webber	Red Bull-Renault	73	+67.3 secs	9	2
8	10	Sebastian Vettel	BMW-Sauber	73	+67.7 secs	7	1
9	3	Giancarlo Fisichella	Renault	72	+1 Lap	10	
10	17	Alexander Wurz	Williams-Toyota	72	+1 Lap	17	

Fastest lap: Kimi Räikkönen, Ferrari: 1:13.117

French Grand Prix

29 June–1 July 2007

Massa takes pole position at Magny-Cours with a lap less than a tenth of a second faster than that of Hamilton. Räikkönen starts from third but Alonso, hit by mechanical problems, will have to work through the field from tenth. In the race, the Ferraris show that they are far better suited to the circuit than the Vodafone McLaren Mercedes. Hamilton is never in the hunt for a third consecutive victory as Räikkönen wins from Massa to revive his championship aspirations. Räikkönen roars past Hamilton at the opening corner and then overhauls Massa during the second round of pit stops. Alonso suffers a frustrating race, never managing to make inroads through the slower cars in front of him, and finishes seventh. Despite Ferrari's dominance, Hamilton extends his championship lead to 14 points and his record run of consecutive podium finishes to eight. He has 64 points, with Alonso on 50, Massa on 47 and Räikkönen on 42.

LEWIS: 'All I saw was Kimi Räikkönen come flying past me in his Ferrari … I thought I was quicker than him in the first part of the race, but sometimes in Formula One you have to be seconds faster to pass someone, so I never had a chance.'

QUALIFYING

Pos	No	Driver	Team	Q1	Q2	Q3
1	5	Felipe Massa	Ferrari	1:15.303	1:14.822	1:15.034
2	2	Lewis Hamilton	McLaren Mercedes	1:14.805	1:14.795	1:15.104
3	6	Kimi Räikkönen	Ferrari	1:14.872	1:14.828	1:15.257
4	10	Robert Kubica	BMW-Sauber	1:15.778	1:15.066	1:15.493
5	3	Giancarlo Fisichella	Renault	1:16.047	1:15.227	1:15.674
6	4	Heikki Kovalainen	Renault	1:15.524	1:15.272	1:15.826
7	9	Nick Heidfeld	BMW-Sauber	1:15.783	1:15.149	1:15.900
8	12	Jarno Trulli	Toyota	1:16.118	1:15.379	1:15.935
9	16	Nico Rosberg	Williams-Toyota	1:16.092	1:15.331	1:16.328
10	1	Fernando Alonso	McLaren Mercedes	1:15.322	1:15.084	

RACE

Pos	No	Driver	Team	Laps	Time/Retired	Grid	Pts
1	6	Kimi Räikkönen	Ferrari	70	1:30:54.200	3	10
2	5	Felipe Massa	Ferrari	70	+2.4 secs	1	8
3	2	Lewis Hamilton	McLaren Mercedes	70	+32.1 secs	2	6
4	10	Robert Kubica	BMW-Sauber	70	+41.7 secs	4	5
5	9	Nick Heidfeld	BMW-Sauber	70	+48.8 secs	7	4
6	3	Giancarlo Fisichella	Renault	70	+52.2 secs	5	3
7	1	Fernando Alonso	McLaren Mercedes	70	+56.5 secs	10	2
8	7	Jenson Button	Honda	70	+58.8 secs	12	1
9	16	Nico Rosberg	Williams-Toyota	70	+68.5 secs	9	
10	11	Ralf Schumacher	Toyota	69	+1 Lap	11	

Fastest lap: Felipe Massa, Ferrari: 1:16.099

Santander British Grand Prix

6–8 July 2007

A record 80,000 Silverstone crowd for qualifying watches Hamilton, the local hero, grab pole position with a dramatic last-gasp flying lap. But on race day, Räikkönen steals the limelight by grabbing his second consecutive victory ahead of Alonso. Hamilton is slightly off the pace and fails to capitalize on a decent early lead. His progress is further hindered by two untidy pit stops. Both Räikkönen and Alonso pass Hamilton during the first round of stops and then move quickly away, leaving the championship leader to a lonely third place. Massa's Ferrari stalls on the grid, forcing him to start the race from the back of the field. He slices through the back markers superbly but can only manage fifth place behind Kubica. After his ninth consecutive podium, Hamilton leaves Silverstone still top of the World Championship with 70 points, ahead of Alonso on 58 and Räikkönen in third on 52.

LEWIS: 'I thought I saw the lollipop move a little bit, but I was wrong ... I let the clutch out too soon ... I had to stop again and it was all a bit of a mess.'

QUALIFYING

Pos	No	Driver	Team	Q1	Q2	Q3
1	2	Lewis Hamilton	McLaren Mercedes	1:19.885	1:19.400	1:19.997
2	6	Kimi Räikkönen	Ferrari	1:19.753	1:19.252	1:20.099
3	1	Fernando Alonso	McLaren Mercedes	1:19.330	1:19.152	1:20.147
4	5	Felipe Massa	Ferrari	1:19.790	1:19.421	1:20.265
5	10	Robert Kubica	BMW-Sauber	1:20.294	1:20.054	1:20.401
6	11	Ralf Schumacher	Toyota	1:20.513	1:19.860	1:20.516
7	4	Heikki Kovalainen	Renault	1:20.570	1:20.077	1:20.721
8	3	Giancarlo Fisichella	Renault	1:20.842	1:20.042	1:20.775
9	9	Nick Heidfeld	BMW-Sauber	1:20.534	1.20.178	1:20.894
10	12	Jarno Trulli	Toyota	1:21.150	1:20.133	1:21.240

RACE

Pos	No	Driver	Team	Laps	Time/Retired	Grid	Pts
1	6	Kimi Räikkönen	Ferrari	59	1:21:43.074	2	10
2	1	Fernando Alonso	McLaren Mercedes	59	+2.4 secs	3	8
3	2	Lewis Hamilton	McLaren Mercedes	59	+39.3 secs	1	6
4	10	Robert Kubica	BMW-Sauber	59	+53.3 secs	4	5
5	5	Felipe Massa	Ferrari	59	+54.0 secs	22	4
6	9	Nick Heidfeld	BMW-Sauber	59	+56.3 secs	8	3
7	4	Helkki Kovalainen	Renault	58	+1 Lap	6	2
8	3	Giancarlo Fisichella	Renault	58	+1 Lap	7	1
9	8	Rubens Barrichello	Honda	58	+1 Lap	13	
10	7	Jenson Button	Honda	58	+1 Lap	17	

Fastest lap: Kimi Räikkönen, Ferrari: 1:20.638

European Grand Prix

20–22 July 2007

A problem with his front right wheel forces Hamilton into a 160 mph crash in qualifying, meaning he starts the race from tenth on the grid. When the session resumes after half an hour, Räikkönen takes pole position. But Räikkönen is forced to retire from the rain-affected race, leaving Massa and Alonso to fight for victory. Alonso eventually comes out on top after overtaking Massa in the closing stages of a thrilling battle. Mark Webber of Red Bull Racing takes a surprise third place. Hamilton's bad luck continues during the race. After moving up to fourth place, he suffers a puncture and is then one of several cars to slide off the track in a sudden torrential downpour. He is placed back onto the track by a crane but his run of podiums ends with a ninth place finish. Alonso's victory closes Hamilton's championship lead to just two points, with Massa a further nine points behind.

LEWIS: 'I saw the two BMWs starting to slide backwards … As I was on the outside, they collided and then Robert was rolling backwards … I could only hope his car would not touch mine, but it did … It left me with a puncture and, from then on, everything became more and more difficult.'

QUALIFYING

Pos	No	Driver	Team	Q1	Q2	Q3
1	6	Kimi Räikkönen	Ferrari	1:31.522	1:31.237	1:31.450
2	1	Fernando Alonso	McLaren Mercedes	1:31.074	1:30.983	1:31.741
3	5	Felipe Massa	Ferrari	1:31.447	1:30.912	1:31.778
4	9	Nick Heidfeld	BMW-Sauber	1:31.889	1:31.652	1:31.840
5	10	Robert Kubica	BMW-Sauber	1:31.961	1:31.444	1:32.123
6	15	Mark Webber	Red Bull-Renault	1:32.629	1:31.661	1:32.476
7	4	Heikki Kovalainen	Renault	1:32.594	1:31.783	1:32.478
8	12	Jarno Trulli	Toyota	1:32.381	1:31.859	1:32.501
9	11	Ralf Schumacher	Toyota	1:32.446	1:31.843	1:32.570
10	2	Lewis Hamilton	McLaren Mercedes	1:31.587	1:31.185	1:33.833

RACE

Pos	No	Driver	Team	Laps	Time/Retired	Grid	Pts
1	1	Fernando Alonso	McLaren Mercedes	60	2:06:26.358	2	10
2	5	Felipe Massa	Ferrari	60	+8.1 secs	3	8
3	15	Mark Webber	Red Bull-Renault	60	+65.6 secs	6	6
4	17	Alexander Wurz	Williams-Toyota	60	+65.9 secs	12	5
5	14	David Coulthard	Red Bull-Renault	60	+73.6 secs	20	4
6	9	Nick Heidfeld	BMW-Sauber	60	+80.2 secs	4	3
7	10	Robert Kubica	BMW-Sauber	60	+82.4 secs	5	2
8	4	Heikki Kovalainen	Renault	59	+1 Lap	7	1
9	2	Lewis Hamilton	McLaren Mercedes	59	+1 Lap	10	
10	3	Giancarlo Fisichella	Renault	59	+1 Lap	13	

Fastest lap: Felipe Massa, Ferrari: 1:32.853

Hungarian Grand Prix

3–5 August 2007

An incident involving Hamilton and Alonso overshadows qualifying for the Grand Prix. Then in the last seconds of the session, Alonso claims pole and Hamilton lacks enough time to respond, leaving him second on the grid. Afterwards, FIA Stewards announce that they will investigate the incident. The outcome is that Vodafone McLaren Mercedes lose any Constructor's Championship points they might earn in the race and Alonso is penalized five grid positions, leaving Hamilton on pole. The tight, twisty circuit produces an uneventful race in which Hamilton holds off Räikkönen to win and Heidfeld takes third place. Alonso finishes fourth. Hamilton moves to 80 points in the championship, ahead of Alonso on 73 and Räikkönen on 60.

LEWIS: 'I started from pole and I knew I had to concentrate and just do my job. I think it worked out reasonably well in the end, but it was not the kind of victory that put a smile on everyone's face.'

QUALIFYING

Pos	No	Driver	Team	Q1	Q2	Q3
1	1	Fernando Alonso	McLaren Mercedes	1:20.425	1:19.661	1:19.674
2	2	Lewis Hamilton	McLaren Mercedes	1:19.570	1.19.301	1:19.781
3	9	Nick Heidfeld	BMW-Sauber	1:20.751	1:20.322	1:20.259
4	6	Kimi Räikkönen	Ferrari	1:20.435	1:20.107	1:20.410
5	16	Nico Rosberg	Williams-Toyota	1:20.547	1:20.188	1:20.632
6	11	Ralf Schumacher	Toyota	1:20.449	1:20.455	1:20.714
7	10	Robert Kubica	BMW-Sauber	1:20.366	1:20.703	1:20.876
8	3	Giancarlo Fisichella	Renault	1:21.645	1:20.590	1:21.079
9	12	Jarno Trulli	Toyota	1:20.481	1:19.951	1:21.206
10	15	Mark Webber	Red Bull-Renault	1:20.794	1:20.439	1:21.256

Note: Alonso and Fisichella were subsequently given five-place grid penalties for impeding another driver.

RACE

Pos	No	Driver	Team	Laps	Time/Retired	Grid	Pts
1	2	Lewis Hamilton	McLaren Mercedes	70	1:35:52.991	1	10
2	6	Kimi Räikkönen	Ferrari	70	+0.7 secs	3	8
3	9	Nick Heidfeld	BMW-Sauber	70	+43.1 secs	2	6
4	1	Fernando Alonso	McLaren Mercedes	70	+44.8 secs	6	5
5	10	Robert Kubica	BMW-Sauber	70	+47.6 secs	7	4
6	11	Ralf Schumacher	Toyota	70	+50.6 secs	5	3
7	16	Nico Rosberg	Williams-Toyota	70	+59.1 secs	4	2
8	4	Heikki Kovalainen	Renault	70	+68.1 secs	11	1
9	15	Mark Webber	Red Bull-Renault	70	+76.3 secs	9	
10	12	Jarno Trulli	Toyota	69	+1 Lap	8	

Fastest lap: Kimi Räikkönen, Ferrari: 1:20.047

Turkish Grand Prix
24–26 August 2007

Massa, winner of the corresponding race last season, takes pole position in Istanbul ahead of Hamilton with Räikkönen third and Alonso fourth. The Brazilian then repeats his 2006 success with an impressive victory, leading from start to finish. Räikkönen and Alonso are second and third respectively. Near the end of the race, Hamilton is running third and seemingly headed for a comfortable podium finish but his left front tyre blows and he is forced to nurse his car round the track on three wheels for an unscheduled pit stop. Alonso and BMW's Nick Heidfeld move past a helpless Hamilton who has to ease his damaged car to the finish, desperately defending a late charge from Heikki Kovalainen to hang on for fifth place. Hamilton moves on to 84 points with Alonso now just five behind on 79. Massa holds third place with 69 points.

LEWIS: '… I was heading for a comfortable podium … until I saw bits of rubber flying off my front right tyre. Then, as I braked for the next corner, it just exploded … The wheel just locked up and I was very lucky I did not end up in the gravel or, even worse, in a wall.'

QUALIFYING

Pos	No	Driver	Team	Q1	Q2	Q3
1	5	Felipe Massa	Ferrari	1:27.488	1:27.039	1:27.329
2	2	Lewis Hamilton	McLaren Mercedes	1:27.513	1:26.936	1:27.373
3	6	Kimi Räikkönen	Ferrari	1:27.294	1:26.902	1:27.546
4	1	Fernando Alonso	McLaren Mercedes	1:27.328	1:26.841	1:27.574
5	10	Robert Kubica	BMW-Sauber	1:27.997	1:27.253	1:27.722
6	9	Nick Heidfeld	BMW-Sauber	1:28.099	1:27.253	1:28.037
7	4	Heikki Kovalainen	Renault	1:28.127	1:27.784	1:28.491
8	16	Nico Rosberg	Williams-Toyota	1:28.275	1:27.750	1:28.501
9	12	Jarno Trulli	Toyota	1:28.318	1:27.801	1:28.740
10	3	Giancarlo Fisichella	Renault	1:28.313	1:27.880	1:29.322

RACE

Pos	No	Driver	Team	Laps	Time/Retired	Grid	Pts
1	5	Felipe Massa	Ferrari	58	1:26:42.161	1	10
2	6	Kimi Räikkönen	Ferrari	58	+2.2 secs	3	8
3	1	Fernando Alonso	McLaren Mercedes	58	+26.1 secs	4	6
4	9	Nick Heidfeld	BMW-Sauber	58	+39.6 secs	6	5
5	2	Lewis Hamilton	McLaren Mercedes	58	+45.0 secs	2	4
6	4	Heikki Kovalainen	Renault	58	+46.1 secs	7	3
7	16	Nico Rosberg	Williams-Toyota	58	+55.7 secs	8	2
8	10	Robert Kubica	BMW-Sauber	58	+56.7 secs	5	1
9	3	Giancarlo Fisichella	Renault	58	+59.4 secs	10	
10	14	David Coulthard	Red Bull-Renault	58	+71.0 secs	13	

Fastest lap: Kimi Räikkönen, Ferrari: 1:27.295

Italian Grand Prix

7–9 September 2007

As the controversy with Ferrari intensifies in the background, Räikkönen escapes with only a stiff neck after a massive crash in practice. The Finn is able to take part in qualifying but is unsurprisingly off form, finishing behind Heidfeld, Massa, Hamilton and Alonso who takes pole position for Vodafone McLaren Mercedes. In front of a partisan Monza crowd the Vodafone McLaren Mercedes drivers keep their cool to complete a one-two in the race at Ferrari's home circuit. Hamilton is unable to prevent Alonso running away with victory and has to pull off a remarkable overtaking manoeuvre to snatch second place from Räikkönen who is eventually third. Räikkönen had slipped past when the rookie made his second pit stop and the Finn seemed surprised when Hamilton immediately moved to take back his position. Alonso's win again closes the gap in the championship race. He is now just three points behind Hamilton with four races remaining. Räikkönen is in third place with 74 points.

LEWIS: 'I knew I only had one shot … I late-braked Kimi at the end of the straight and took my second place back. That is where I finished in the end, which was respectable.'

QUALIFYING

Pos	No	Driver	Team	Q1	Q2	Q3
1	1	Fernando Alonso	McLaren Mercedes	1:21.718	1:21.356	1:21.997
2	2	Lewis Hamilton	McLaren Mercedes	1:21.956	1:21.746	1:22.034
3	5	Felipe Massa	Ferrari	1:22.309	1:21.993	1:22.549
4	9	Nick Heidfeld	BMW-Sauber	1:23.107	1:22.466	1:23.174
5	6	Kimi Räikkönen	Ferrari	1:22.673	1:22.369	1:23.103
6	10	Robert Kubica	BMW-Sauber	1:23.088	1:22.400	1:23.446
7	4	Heikki Kovalainen	Renault	1:23.505	1:23.134	1:24.102
8	16	Nico Rosberg	Williams-Toyota	1:23.333	1:22.748	1:24.382
9	12	Jarno Trulli	Toyota	1:23.724	1:23.107	1:24.555
10	7	Jenson Button	Honda	1:23.639	1:23.021	1:25.165

RACE

Pos	No	Driver	Team	Laps	Time/Retired	Grid	Pts
1	1	Fernando Alonso	McLaren Mercedes	53	1:18:37.806	1	10
2	2	Lewis Hamilton	McLaren Mercedes	53	+6.0 secs	2	8
3	6	Kimi Räikkönen	Ferrari	53	+27.3 secs	5	6
4	9	Nick Heidfeld	BMW-Sauber	53	+56.5 secs	4	5
5	10	Robert Kubica	BMW-Sauber	53	+60.5 secs	6	4
6	16	Nico Rosberg	Williams-Toyota	53	+65.8 secs	8	3
7	4	Heikki Kovalainen	Renault	53	+66.7 secs	7	2
8	7	Jenson Button	Honda	53	+72.1 secs	10	1
9	15	Mark Webber	Red Bull-Renault	53	+75.8 secs	11	
10	8	Rubens Barrichello	Honda	53	+76.9 secs	12	

Fastest lap: Fernando Alonso, Vodafone McLaren Mercedes: 1:22.871

Belgian Grand Prix
14–16 September 2007

Ferrari have the edge on the track at Spa-Francorchamps. Räikkönen and Massa take the front row in qualifying, Vodafone McLaren Mercedes having to settle for the second row with Alonso just ahead of Hamilton. Ferrari dominate the race, Räikkönen securing a third consecutive win at the legendary circuit. Massa is second, Alonso third and Hamilton fourth. The post-race intrigue focuses on a first-corner exchange between Hamilton and Alonso. Hamilton had had the better start and as he tried to overtake his team-mate, Alonso cut across, forcing him to take evasive action and swerve temporarily off the track. The manoeuvre forced Hamilton to yield and he never had another opportunity to challenge for third place. Although Alonso and the race Stewards saw the move as a fair one, Hamilton disagreed. The title race heads to Asia with Hamilton leading the championship on 97 points from Alonso on 95 with Räikkönen on 84.

LEWIS: 'As we exited La Source, he [Alonso] swung his car out across mine and effectively forced me off the track. He left me no room whatsoever … There was plenty of room for both of us and he deliberately pushed me as wide as he could.'

QUALIFYING

Pos	No	Driver	Team	Q1	Q2	Q3
1	6	Kimi Räikkönen	Ferrari	1:46.242	1:45.070	1:45.994
2	5	Felipe Massa	Ferrari	1:46.060	1:45.173	1:46.011
3	1	Fernando Alonso	McLaren Mercedes	1:46.058	1:45.442	1:46.091
4	**2**	**Lewis Hamilton**	**McLaren Mercedes**	**1:46.437**	**1:45.132**	**1:46.406**
5	10	Robert Kubica	BMW-Sauber	1:46.707	1:45.885	1:46.996
6	16	Nico Rosberg	Williams-Toyota	1:46.950	1:46.469	1:47.334
7	9	Nick Heidfeld	BMW-Sauber	1:46.923	1:45.994	1:47.409
8	15	Mark Webber	Red Bull-Renault	1:47.084	1:46.426	1:47.524
9	12	Jarno Trulli	Toyota	1:47.143	1:46.480	1:47.798
10	4	Heikki Kovalainen	Renault	1:46.971	1:46.240	1:48.505

RACE

Pos	No	Driver	Team	Laps	Time/Retired	Grid	Pts
1	6	Kimi Räikkönen	Ferrari	44	1:20:39.066	1	10
2	5	Felipe Massa	Ferrari	44	+4.6 secs	2	8
3	1	Fernando Alonso	McLaren Mercedes	44	+14.3 secs	3	6
4	**2**	**Lewis Hamilton**	**McLaren Mercedes**	**44**	**+23.6 secs**	**4**	**5**
5	9	Nick Heidfeld	BMW-Sauber	44	+51.8 secs	6	4
6	16	Nico Rosberg	Williams-Toyota	44	+76.8 secs	5	3
7	15	Mark Webber	Red Bull-Renault	44	+80.6 secs	7	2
8	4	Heikki Kovalainen	Renault	44	+85.1 secs	9	1
9	10	Robert Kubica	BMW-Sauber	44	+85.6 secs	14	
10	11	Ralf Schumacher	Toyota	44	+88.5 secs	10	

Fastest lap: Felipe Massa, Ferrari: 1:48.036

Japanese Grand Prix
28–30 September 2007

Hamilton takes pole position in the wet at Fuji ahead of Alonso, Räikkönen and Massa. Forty-two laps into the race, Alonso loses control of his Vodafone McLaren Mercedes and crashes into a wall. Hamilton, meanwhile, survives an aggressive overtaking move from Kubica who is later penalized by Stewards for nudging Hamilton off the track temporarily. Mark Webber and Sebastian Vettel are forced to retire from the race after clashing in a Safety Car period, allowing Renault's Heikki Kovalainen to finish second and Räikkönen third. Räikkönen and Massa (who was eventually sixth) were handicapped by having to pit on the second lap after starting on intermediate tyres rather than the 'extreme' wets demanded by race officials. Hamilton's win stretches his championship lead over Alonso to twelve points with Räikkönen a further five points back in third.

LEWIS: 'Like everyone else in that race, I was under a lot of pressure to look after my car, my brakes, and deal with the conditions.'

QUALIFYING

Pos	No	Driver	Team	Q1	Q2	Q3
1	2	Lewis Hamilton	McLaren Mercedes	1:25.489	1:24.753	1:25.368
2	1	Fernando Alonso	McLaren Mercedes	1:25.379	1:24.806	1:25.438
3	6	Kimi Räikkönen	Ferrari	1:25.390	1:24.988	1:25.516
4	5	Felipe Massa	Ferrari	1:25.359	1:25.049	1:25.765
5	9	Nick Heidfeld	BMW-Sauber	1:25.971	1:25.248	1:26.505
6	16	Nico Rosberg	Williams-Toyota	1:26.579	1:25.816	1:26.728
7	7	Jenson Button	Honda	1:26.614	1:25.454	1:26.913
8	15	Mark Webber	Red Bull-Renault	1:25.970	1:25.535	1:26.914
9	19	Sebastian Vettel	STR-Ferrari	1:26.025	1:25.909	1:26.973
10	10	Robert Kubica	BMW-Sauber	1:26.300	1:25.530	1:27.225

RACE

Pos	No	Driver	Team	Laps	Time/Retired	Grid	Pts
1	2	Lewis Hamilton	McLaren Mercedes	67	2:00:34.579	1	10
2	4	Heikki Kovalainen	Renault	67	+8.3 secs	11	8
3	6	Kimi Räikkönen	Ferrari	67	+9.4 secs	3	6
4	14	David Coulthard	Red Bull-Renault	67	+20.2 secs	12	5
5	3	Giancarlo Fisichella	Renault	67	+38.8 secs	10	4
6	5	Felipe Massa	Ferrari	67	+49.0 secs	4	3
7	10	Robert Kubica	BMW-Sauber	67	+49.2 secs	9	2
8	20	Adrian Sutil	Spyker-Ferrari	67	+60.1 secs	19	1
9	18	Vitantonio Liuzzi	STR-Ferrari	67	+80.6 secs	22	
10	8	Rubens Barrichello	Honda	67	+88.3 secs	16	

Note: Liuzzi finished eighth, but had 25 seconds added to his time for passing under yellow flags.

Fastest lap: Lewis Hamilton, Vodafone McLaren Mercedes: 1:28.193

Chinese Grand Prix

5–7 October 2007

Hamilton seems to take a major step towards the championship by taking pole position in Shanghai. Räikkönen is second fastest in qualifying, with Alonso only fourth on the grid behind Massa. But the title race takes another twist in the rain-affected Grand Prix. Hamilton establishes a substantial early lead but, as his tyres wear on the drying track, he is clawed back by Räikkönen who manages to overtake on lap 29. Then, shortly afterwards, Hamilton suffers a disaster. As he enters the pit lane to change his now seriously bald tyres, Hamilton slides off the track and into a gravel trap. It is the rookie's first retirement of the season. Alonso takes advantage of his team-mate's misfortune to claim second place and take the championship to the final race. Massa is third for Ferrari. Hamilton now leads with 107 points from Alonso's 103, with Räikkönen on 100 points.

LEWIS: 'I started turning into the pit lane corner and … just lost the back end. I had good front tyres but just no rears at all … I wasn't to know it was going to be just like an ice rink and that I was going to go off and get stuck in the only gravel trap in a pit lane in the whole world.'

QUALIFYING

Pos	No	Driver	Team	Q1	Q2	Q3
1	2	Lewis Hamilton	McLaren Mercedes	1:35.798	1:35.898	1:35.908
2	6	Kimi Räikkönen	Ferrari	1:35.692	1:35.381	1:36.044
3	5	Felipe Massa	Ferrari	1:35.792	1:35.796	1:36.221
4	1	Fernando Alonso	McLaren Mercedes	1:35.809	1:35.845	1:36.576
5	14	David Coulthard	Red Bull-Renault	1:36.930	1:36.252	1:37.619
6	11	Ralf Schumacher	Toyota	1:37.135	1:36.709	1:38.013
7	15	Mark Webber	Red Bull-Renault	1:37.199	1:36.602	1:38.153
8	9	Nick Heidfeld	BMW-Sauber	1:36.737	1:36.217	1:38.455
9	10	Robert Kubica	BMW-Sauber	1:36.309	1:36.116	1:38.472
10	7	Jenson Button	Honda	1:37.092	1:36.771	1:39.285

RACE

Pos	No	Driver	Team	Laps	Time/Retired	Grid	Pts
1	6	Kimi Räikkönen	Ferrari	56	1:37:58.395	2	10
2	1	Fernando Alonso	McLaren Mercedes	56	+9.8 secs	4	8
3	5	Felipe Massa	Ferrari	56	+12.8 secs	3	6
4	19	Sebastian Vettel	STR-Ferrari	56	+53.5 secs	17	5
5	7	Jenson Button	Honda	56	+68.6 secs	10	4
6	18	Vitantonio Liuzzi	STR-Ferrari	56	+73.6 secs	11	3
7	9	Nick Heidfeld	BMW-Sauber	56	+74.2 secs	8	2
8	14	David Coulthard	Red Bull-Renault	56	+80.7 secs	5	1
9	4	Heikki Kovalainen	Renault	56	+81.1 secs	13	
10	15	Mark Webber	Red Bull-Renault	56	+84.6 secs	7	

Fastest lap: Felipe Massa, Ferrari: 1:37.454

Brazilian Grand Prix

19–21 October 2007

Felipe Massa takes pole position in front of his adoring home crowd, edging out Hamilton by less than two-tenths of a second. Räikkönen is third on the grid ahead of Alonso. In the race Kimi Räikkönen takes the 2007 Drivers' Championship in the most dramatic style possible. Räikkönen is helped by his Ferrari colleague Massa who leads much of the race before moving aside for his team-mate to take the glory. Alonso finishes third but the Spaniard is never able to compete with the Ferraris. He finishes the season a single point behind Räikkönen, as does Hamilton who suffers a poor start and slips down to fourth place, behind Räikkönen and Alonso, by the first corner. He then tries to re-pass Alonso and ends up off the track, rejoining in eighth place. There is further drama eight laps into the race as Hamilton suffers a gearbox problem that costs him 40 seconds and, as it turns out, the World Championship. The rookie switches to a three-stop strategy and battles to make positions from the rear of the field but despite his best efforts can only finish seventh.

Lewis: 'The car lost its drive and I was stuck in neutral, just coasting as I downshifted going into turn four, the Subida da Lago, again. In a flash, I could see everything passing me – all the other cars, the whole season, everything we had done.'

QUALIFYING

Pos	No	Driver	Team	Q1	Q2	Q3
1	5	Felipe Massa	Ferrari	1:12.303	1:12.374	1:11.931
2	2	Lewis Hamilton	McLaren-Mercedes	1:13.033	1:12.296	1:12.082
3	6	Kimi Räikkönen	Ferrari	1:13.016	1:12.161	1:12.322
4	1	Fernando Alonso	McLaren-Mercedes	1:12.895	1:12.637	1:12.956
5	15	Mark Webber	Red Bull-Renault	1:13.081	1:12.683	1:12.928
6	9	Nick Heidfeld	BMW-Sauber	1:13.472	1:12.888	1:13.081
7	10	Robert Kubica	BMW-Sauber	1:13.085	1:12.641	1:13.129
8	12	Jarno Trulli	Toyota	1:13.470	1:12.832	1:13.195
9	14	David Coulthard	Red Bull-Renault	1:13.264	1:12.846	1:13.272
10	16	Nico Rosberg	Williams-Toyota	1:13.707	1:12.752	1:13.477

RACE

Pos	No	Driver	Team	Laps	Time/Retired	Grid	Pts
1	6	Kimi Räikkönen	Ferrari	71	1:28:15.270	3	10
2	5	Felipe Massa	Ferrari	71	+1.4 secs	1	8
3	1	Fernando Alonso	McLaren-Mercedes	71	+57.0 secs	4	6
4	16	Nico Rosberg	Williams-Toyota	71	+62.8 secs	10	5
5	10	Robert Kubica	BMW-Sauber	71	+70.9 secs	7	4
6	9	Nick Heidfeld	BMW-Sauber	71	+71.3 secs	6	3
7	2	Lewis Hamilton	McLaren-Mercedes	70	+1 Lap	2	2
8	12	Jarno Trulli	Toyota	70	+1 Lap	8	1
9	14	David Coulthard	Red Bull-Renault	70	+1 Lap	9	
10	17	Kazuki Nakajima	Williams-Toyota	70	+1 Lap	19	

Fastest lap: Kimi Räikkönen, Ferrari: 1:12.445

2007 FORMULA ONE SEASON SUMMARY

Drivers' Championship

Pos	Driver	Nationality	Team	Points
1	Kimi Räikkönen	Finnish	Ferrari	110
2	**Lewis Hamilton**	**British**	**McLaren Mercedes**	**109**
3	Fernando Alonso	Spanish	McLaren Mercedes	109
4	Felipe Massa	Brazilian	Ferrari	94
5	Nick Heidfeld	German	BMW-Sauber	61
6	Robert Kubica	Polish	BMW-Sauber	39
7	Heikki Kovalainen	Finnish	Renault	30
8	Giancarlo Fisichella	Italian	Renault	21
9	Nico Rosberg	German	Williams-Toyota	20
10	David Coulthard	British	Red Bull-Renault	14
11	Alexander Wurz	Austrian	Williams-Toyota	13
12	Mark Webber	Australian	Red Bull-Renault	10
13	Jarno Trulli	Italian	Toyota	8
14	Sebastian Vettel	German	STR-Ferrari	6
15	Jenson Button	British	Honda	6
16	Ralf Schumacher	German	Toyota	5
17	Takuma Sato	Japanese	Super Aguri-Honda	4
18	Vitantonio Liuzzi	Italian	STR-Ferrari	3
19	Adrian Sutil	German	Spyker-Ferrari	1
20	Rubens Barrichello	Brazilian	Honda	0
21	Scott Speed	USA	STR-Ferrari	0
22	Kazuki Nakajima	Japanese	Williams-Toyota	0
23	Anthony Davidson	British	Super Aguri-Honda	0
24	Sakon Yamamoto	Japanese	Spyker-Ferrari	0
25	Christijan Albers	Dutch	Spyker-Ferrari	0
26	Markus Winkelhock	German	Spyker-Ferrari	0

Constructors' Championship

Pos	Team	Points
1	Ferrari	204
2	BMW-Sauber	101
3	Renault	51
4	Williams-Toyota	33
5	Red Bull-Renault	24
6	Toyota	13
7	STR-Ferrari	8
8	Honda	6
9	Super Aguri-Honda	4
10	Spyker-Ferrari	1
-	McLaren Mercedes	0

Note: McLaren stripped of all constructors' points for 2007 following a decision of the World Motor Sports Council on 13 September 2007.

Race-by-race driver points

	Hamilton		Räikkönen		Alonso		Massa	
	race	cumulative	race	cumulative	race	cumulative	race	cumulative
Australian	6	6	10	10	8	8	3	3
Malaysian	8	14	6	16	10	18	4	7
Bahrain	8	22	6	22	4	22	10	17
Spanish	8	30	0	22	6	28	10	27
Monaco	8	38	1	23	10	38	6	33
Canadian	10	48	4	27	2	40	0	33
United States	10	58	5	32	8	48	6	39
French	6	64	10	42	2	50	8	47
British	6	70	10	52	8	58	4	51
European	0	70	0	52	10	68	8	59
Hungarian	10	80	8	60	5	73	0	59
Turkish	4	84	8	68	6	79	10	69
Italian	8	92	6	74	10	89	0	69
Belgian	5	97	10	84	6	95	8	77
Japanese	10	107	6	90	0	95	3	80
Chinese	0	107	10	100	8	103	6	86
Brazilian	2	109	10	110	6	109	8	94

INDEX

PICTURE CREDITS

(t = top, c = centre, b = bottom, l = left, r = right; numbers refer to plate pages)

ACTION IMAGES: 26b (REUTERS/Umit Bektas), 28t (REUTERS/HO-FIA), 29br (Crispin Thruston Livepic)

ANGLIA PRESS AGENCY LTD/REX FEATURES: 2br, 7b

RUSSELL BATCHELOR: 12–13, 14b, 21tl

PAUL-HENRI CAHIER: 14t, 22t, 28b

DPII: 18c (Gilles Levent), 19bl (Eric Vargiolu)

EPA: 13cl (Roland Weihrauch), 22br (Kerim Okten), 27bl (Carmen Jasperson), 29bl (Kerim Okten)

GETTY IMAGES: 22cr (Mark Thompson), 24 inset (Marcus Brandt/AFP), 25 (Mark Thompson), 26tl (Getty Images Sport), 30c (Vladimir Rys/Bongarts), 31b (Clive Mason), 32b (Vanderlei Almeida/AFP)

HOCH ZWEI: 9 (Juergen Tap), 12b (Michael Kunkel), 22cl (Juergen Tap), 22bl (Juergen Tap), 27c (Michael Kunkel), 30b (Juergen Tap), 31c (Juergen Tap), back endpaper reverse (Juergen Tap)

LAT PHOTOGRAPHIC: 10bl (Glenn Dunbar), 11tl (Andrew Ferraro/GP2 Series Media Services), 11tr (Lorenzo Bellanca/GP2 Series Media Services), 11c (Glenn Dunbar/GP2 Series Media Services), 13c (Steve Etherington), 13b (Andrew

Ferraro), 14–15 (Steven Tee), 16 (Steven Tee), 18t (Charles Coates), 18bl (Steven Tee), 18br (Lorenzo Bellanca), 19br (Andrew Ferraro), 20–21 (Andrew Ferraro), 21c (Glenn Dunbar), 22–23, 25, 26c (Steven Tee), 27t, 27br (Steve Etherington), 28–29 (Steven Tee), 31t (Lorenzo Bellanca), 32t (Charles Coates), back endpaper (Steve Etherington), chapter opener cutouts 12, 44, 60

NI SYNDICATION: 19t

PA PHOTOS: 3cr (Sutton), 5tl (Kieran Doherty/PA Archive)

RACING LINE MAGAZINE: 5tr (Laurence Baker/Chris Dixon), 6 (Phil Meech), 8 (Hugo Dixon), 12t (Hugo Dixon), 17 (Mitch Jenkins)

SCHLEGELMILCH PHOTOGRAPHY: 12c

JAD SHERIF: 9, 15t, 15c

SUTTON-IMAGES.COM: 3c, 3cl, 5b, 5 (inset), 10t, 10cl, 10cr, 10br, 10bc, 11b, 24 (all), 31 (inset)

WWW.MCLAREN.COM/HOCH ZWEI: front endpaper, 21tr

Front cover photograph: Lewis Hamilton is dressed in BOSS black.

All other photographs supplied courtesy of Lewis Hamilton.